The Bristol Downs
a natural history year

Geraldine Taylor

Dru Marland
Illustrator

Mandy Leivers
Natural history consultant

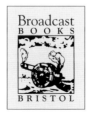

Broadcast
BOOKS

BRISTOL

© 2008 Geraldine Taylor

Published by Broadcast Books
7 Exeter Buildings, Bristol BS6 6TH
catherine@broadcastbooks.co.uk
www.broadcastbooks.co.uk
Tel: 0117 923 8891

Illustrations © 2008 Dru Marland

Designed by Martin Laurie
martinlaurie@ukonline.co.uk
Tel: 01925 757 864

Printed and bound by
Henry Ling Limited
The Dorset Press, Dorchester
Dorset, DT1 1HD

Isbn: 978 1 874092 52 0

*To the memory of my beloved mum and dad
and gran: and the extraordinary childhood that
made my love of wildlife possible.*

Geraldine Taylor

Contents

Introduction

By Mandy Leivers

For many people the Downs are a treasured and much-loved location, where you can walk the dog, fly a kite, enjoy a picnic or simply unwind. They're also perfect for wildlife watching.

'The Bristol Downs – a natural history year' is a wonderful book! Geraldine's insightful observations are so evocative that it makes me want to rush out onto the Downs and experience the things she's seen for myself. Some of her descriptions make me gasp because she's captured a moment so beautifully, some make me laugh out loud, and others fill me with joy. All make me vow to pay more attention in the future.

We're very lucky to have so much wildlife on the Downs and to have Geraldine to observe and share it with us. I hope you enjoy this journey through the changing seasons as much as I have. Let Geraldine guide you. Get out there and enjoy the wildlife of the Downs for yourself!

Mandy Leivers
Avon Gorge and Downs Biodiversity Education Officer

The Avon Gorge & Downs Wildlife Project

The Avon Gorge & Downs Wildlife Project is working to secure the outstanding wildlife interest of the Avon Gorge and Clifton and Durdham Downs. We also aim to raise awareness and understanding about the importance of this site for people and wildlife.

The Project is a partnership of Bristol City Council, Bristol Zoo Gardens, Natural England, the Society of Merchant Venturers, the Downs Committee and Bristol University. We are also working with the National Trust who manage part of Leigh Woods, on the north Somerset side of the Gorge.

We have three areas to our work:

Wildlife surveying and monitoring – This work is carried out by local ecologists, often using climbing techniques to access certain areas of the Gorge.

Habitat management work – We are working to protect the species-rich grassland areas in the Gorge and on the Downs. The meadow areas on the Downs are also left unmown during the spring and summer to allow the plants in these areas to flower and set seed.

Education – We provide opportunities for everyone to discover more about and enjoy the wildlife and the landscape of the Gorge and Downs. As part of this aim we run a very popular programme of walks, talks, courses and children's holiday activities. We also run educational trips to the Downs for school groups. A range of nature trail leaflets is also available.

For further information visit www.avongorge.org.uk
or call 0117 9030609

Lime

The View From
The Edge of the Gorge

By John Maher

"As I arrived at the Peregrine Watch and peered over the
edge for the foxes, I noticed a kestrel land in one of the
ash trees beside the road, he didn't stop long, but swooped
down onto the newly cut grass; there was a flutter of wings
as he caught – something – probably a vole or mouse
– and was off. Apart from several squadrons of mallard,
a duo of cormorants, and numerous seagulls, crows and
jackdaws, a solitary redshank, not much!"

http://morningbikeride.blogspot.com/ 17-4-08

The event described took all of thirty seconds, and illustrates the
fact that, for the observant, there is always something to see if you
trouble to walk over to the Gorge and look down onto the Avon estuary.
Somehow, there is often more to see if there are muddy fringes to the
river, always mallard, flying, dabbling at the river edges, or being swept
along with the tide. Pigeons moving with rapid wing beats across the
Gorge; jackdaws, invariably in pairs, playing in the wind, or perching in
'their' tree.

Then there are redshank. These line the mud, walking, running, head
bobbing back and forth, or pecking for marine worms. The redshank walk
the water edge, singly during the autumn and winter months, forming
small groups in spring and summer. If you are lucky you will see them fly
low over the water, the white flashes from the back edges to their wings
catch the sun, just as their eponymous red legs give their identity away.
There are other visitors, sometimes oystercatcher, curlew, and heron. The

cormorants can be seen on rocks exposed at low tide, wings stretched in a Batman-like pose as they digest their catch. Many kinds of gull: greater and lesser black-backed, herring gull, common gull, and, especially in winter, large numbers of black-headed gulls. Watch the plumage of the black-headed gulls; in summer they have little black or brown caps that disappear during the winter months, replaced by dark patches that make them look as if they are wearing headphones!

Let your eyes wander up to the edge of Leigh Woods, a small lantern-like speck in an oak may be one of the peregrines. On the cliff opposite the Peregrine Watch is the ravens' nest; in spring small black heads appear, and the adults come back and forth feeding their brood. The ravens are as majestic in flight as are buzzards, usually sighted high above the Gorge. Even higher again, the peregrines, sometimes a thousand feet up – watch for a 200 miles-an-hour swoop onto an unfortunate feral or wood pigeon. If the peregrine hits the pigeon, a cloud of feathers may erupt, and after, the peregrine has to be careful not to land where one of the ravens can see her – and steal the catch. Sometimes the peregrines can be seen skimming the trees, more like a sparrowhawk. A peregrine coming into the nest below the Peregrine Watch moves fast, and you need to be at the very edge for a glimpse. Sparrowhawks, yes, as well as the kestrel, maybe even a goshawk, red kite or even an osprey! Mobile jewels that inhabit Bristol's greatest glory – the Avon Gorge.

Redshank

The Bristol Downs: Geology and History

By Dru Marland

The Bristol Downs are part of a limestone ridge which extends north-eastwards from Clevedon. It was formed by sedimentation and deposition when a tropical sea spread over the area during the early Carboniferous period, 354 million years ago. Fossils of marine creatures can be seen where the rock is exposed. During the Hercynian period (about 290 million years ago), when the ancient continents of Laurasia and Gondwana collided, this rock was folded and pushed up into mountains. It was then eroded, deposited upon, uplifted and again eroded until the present surface was once more exposed.

The Gorge was created during the Ice Ages which have come and gone over the last two million years. Bristol itself escaped glaciation, but an ice sheet advanced from Ireland up into the Bristol Channel, reaching the Failand Ridge just to the west. It is probable that the Avon cut its way through the Downs because it had been impeded in its original westward flow through Ashton Vale and beyond by this advancing ice front. In the interglacial periods, animals such as bears, elephants, horses, rhinos and hyaenas inhabited the area. Remains of these animals were found in a quarry in Durdham Down in 1842; today part of this discovery (hyaena and elephant bones) can be seen at the City Museum, along with some stone tools of our ancestors, showing that they too were present. The Downs would have been covered with mixed woodland, except in the steeper and rockier areas which would have been colonised by grasses and scrub, much as they are today.

Tree felling began as long as 4000 years ago, and there are field systems evident between Ladies Mile and the Zoo Banks. During the Iron Age, the Dobunni tribe built a hill fort on Observatory Hill, which, together with the two forts on the Leigh Woods side of the Gorge, dominated the river. The Romans in turn built villas in the area, and the road which they built, linking Bath with the port of Abonae (Sea Mills), can still be traced near Stoke Road. The Saxons established grazing rights on the Downs and left boundary stones from Walcombe Slade (Black Rock Gully) to the Water Tower. By the time of William the Conqueror, The Domesday Book of 1086 records the Manor of Clifton as having a population of thirty, of whom half were farm labourers. The Downs provided grazing for the commoners of Clifton and Henbury, and land was leased by the Lords of the Manors for quarrying, lead mining, and limekilns.

The Downs witnessed some turbulence over the centuries. The Royalist army grouped here before taking the city in 1643, and then the Parliamentarians did the same thing two years later. For centuries this was not an area to cross after nightfall because of the footpads and highwaymen, who, if caught, were suspended from the gibbet at the top of Pembroke Road – or Gallows Acre Lane as it was known until the 1850s. With the advent of turnpikes, a tollbooth was installed at the top of Bridge Valley Road in 1727, and then attacked by rioting miners. More recently, troops were stationed here during both world wars, and the Second World War saw the erection of stone obstacles to prevent the landing of enemy aircraft, the tethering of barrage balloons, and the positioning of an anti-aircraft battery at the Dumps. With the arrival of American troops, the Downs were used as a vehicle assembly area in

readiness for D Day, and wild flowers flourished between tanks in this temporary respite from mowing.

More of a threat to the Downs, though, was encroaching development. Clifton became a fashionable place of resort with the development of Hotwells as a spa in the late 17th century. John Evelyn described a hunt for Bristol Diamonds (quartz geodes) in 1654:

> *What was most stupendous to me, was the rock of St Vincent, a little distance from the Towne, the precipice whereof is equal to any thing of that nature I have seene in the most confragose cataracts of the Alpes: The river gliding between them after an extraordinary depth: Here we went searching for Diamonds, & to the hot Well at its foote...*

Although development faltered with Hotwell's decline, by the 19th century it had again revived with the expanding and affluent middle classes seeking to escape from the noxious industrial heart of the city in the valley of the Frome to the fresher air of the suburbs near the Downs. Quarrying, mining, clay extraction and illicit enclosure all caused further public concern at the loss of the Downs as an amenity for all the citizens of Bristol. The City bought Durdham Down from the Lords of the Manor of Henbury and, along with the Merchant Venturers who owned the Clifton Downs, obtained an Act of Parliament in 1861 to ensure free public access. Plans were enacted for the 'beautification' of the Downs. The Circular Road was built, quarry workings were filled in, and avenues of trees planted. Change also came about by the decline in sheep grazing, which had hitherto kept in check the growth in trees and scrub; it died out on Clifton Down in the 19th century, and effectively ended in 1925 on Durdham Down, although the University of Bristol, and other Downs Commoners, continue to graze a small number of sheep here every ten years in order to protect their rights, the last time being in 2006.

The fact that the Downs have survived to give pleasure to generation after generation of Bristolians is a mixture of happy historical accident and the unusual foresight of the city officials. Today, management of the Downs is the responsibility of the Downs Committee and Downs Ranger, whose work ensures the preservation of this beautiful, much-loved open space for generations of Bristolians to come.

Flora and Fauna

Flowers

We're never without wild flowers on the Bristol Downs. Even in the depth of winter, there will be a smattering of frosted daisies and some purple sweet violets. This is a small, personal selection.

Agrimony (*Agrimonia eupatoria*)

Flowering time late June–September.
Locations Circular Road meadow; Zoo Banks; Can occur anywhere.
See Walk July B.

Agrimony has a rocket trail of yellow flowers, and the fragrance of apricots. The spike is 30–60cm high, but the many five-petalled yellow stars are less than 1cm across.

Agrimony is derived from *Argemone*, a name given by the Greeks to plants that healed the eyes.

The plant was also associated with magic and was known as *fairy's wand* in SW England. The modern magic of this lovely flower is that it seems able to appear anywhere on the Downs.

Autumn lady's tresses (*Spiranthes spiralis*)

Flowering time August–September.
Locations Circular Road meadows, but be alert for them anywhere.
See Walk August A.

Autumn lady's tresses orchids have recently reappeared on the Downs. I saw them many years ago, in short turf, fairly near their current site. The plant is a slow grower, taking eleven years from seed for the first leaves to be formed, and then several years more for flowers to be produced.

This is the last orchid of the year to appear in Bristol. It's so small and white that it's easily overlooked until you get your eye in.

Tiny white and green flowers spiral like a plait around a spike 5–15cm high. The rosette of blue-green leaves, produced in June, dies before the spike arises in August to September.

The flowers are scented, and in common with the butterfly orchid (which can be found in Leigh Woods) this is especially strong in the evening. The scent is variously described as being like honey, almonds and old plimsolls.

All parts of flower spike are covered with minute white hairs, and the plant looks rather frosty.

Bee orchid (*Ophrys apifera*)

Flowering time late May–June.
Locations meadow areas.
See Walk June A.

Bee orchids are the meadows' greatest treasure. The single stems are of moderate height (15–30cm) but surprisingly hard to find. Best to look at the same time each day – a change of light can make them invisible: I've been driven to despair. Leaves are unspotted and oval, and their cool green often gives the plant away.

See one bee orchid to understand the passion of orchid lovers. The realistic 'bee' is the lip of the flower; it's velvet to the touch. The latest evidence, taken from pollen on the fossilised remains of a bee, is that the orchid family may have co-existed with dinosaurs – appearing between 76 million and 84 million years ago.

Look, too, for wasps on a stalk. The wasp orchid is nationally rare but locally plentiful in the Gorge. So far, I've found three of these in the meadow grass on the Downs

Bird's-foot-trefoil (Lotus corniculatus)

Flowering time May–September.
Locations The Dumps; meadow grass areas,
including the White Tree Meadow;
Zoo Banks; Observatory Hill.
See Walk June A.

Bird's-foot-trefoil grows abundantly on the Bristol
Downs. Richard Jefferies* writes *The bird's-foot-lotus is the
picture to me of sunshine and summer*. Certainly, it's widely beloved, with
over 70 folk names. I always smile when I see it.

The sweet-smelling yellow flower is carried on a stalked head. It
resembles a bird's claw, but occasional vivid streaks of red or orange
suggest a different name: *bacon-and-eggs*. Buds and dying petals can be
poppy red.

Small leaves are formed in threes, with a further leaflet close to the
flower. Bird's-foot-trefoil is a larval food plant of the common blue
butterfly: the butterfly itself can often be seen feeding on the flowers,
and the yellow and blue is a beautiful colour combination.

* Wild Flowers in *Under the Acorns*

Black knapweed (Centaurea nigra)

Flowering time late June–September.
Locations meadow areas.
See Walk July B.

Black knapweed flowers are welcome points
of rosy purple in the meadows. They are soft, lightly
fragrant flowers – thistle-like (they are part of the thistle
family) but without prickles, and tall (40–70cm). The
flowers sit on top of dark and pale brown globes of bracts.
The folk name of this flower is *hard heads* and a gentle squeeze of the
bracts will demonstrate why.

The bonus of black knapweed is the source of nectar it offers, appealing to butterflies, bees, hoverflies and burnet moths. On the Downs, I've seen small tortoiseshell, peacock, brimstone, meadow brown and marbled white butterflies on the flower heads, the latter – purple, and black and white – being a spectacular colour combination.

Bluebell (*Hyacinthoides non-scripta*)

Flowering time   April–May.
Locations   Fairyland Woods; Zoo Banks.
See Walk   April B.

Bluebells can be found scattered around the Downs. Not the massed inky intensity of some regions of Leigh Woods across the Gorge, but sufficient to give a flavour of bluebell time. Bluebells are as varied as snowflakes. On the Downs, I've found flowering stems measuring 8cm, and others 40cm tall. Some have a single bell and others have up to 30. Bluebells are striped and the combination of these stripes (usually blue and lilac, often kingfisher) gives the flower its electric colour. Open bells are lighter, closed bells almost purple or navy.

The bottom bell is the first to flower. The stem bends to its fluid arc and there's a detectable fragrance when at least two bells are open. The scent is strongest in the sun after rain.

Some of the Downs' bluebells have hybridised with the introduced Spanish bluebell (*H. hispanica*) – and these are more of a washed out colour. and coarser and straighter – without the arc which gives our bluebells their compliant sway in the wind.

Common rock-rose (Helianthemum nummularium)

Flowering time May–September.
Locations The Dumps; Zoo Banks and Woods; Clifton Down meadow areas, especially around the Circular Road.
See Walk June A.

Rock-roses are better not touched as the tissue-like yellow petals are frail and quickly detach: I'm surprised that the flowers survive the high winds on the Downs. Lacking scent, the tiny (2cm in diameter) flower has glorious colour and pattern. The buds have an oriental, lantern-like beauty, and the stamens form an orange core in the matt yellow of the open flower. These stamens are sensitive and if brushed by the wing of an insect, lie down on the petals as though flabbergasted: I tested this with a feather.

The leaves are small, paired along the stem, and hairy. Rock-roses rarely grow alone, often keeping company with bird's-foot-trefoil, thyme, salad burnet, eyebright, tormentil and yellow rattle.

The flower closes at night and when it's wet to keep its pollen dry, hence its folk name *Sun rose*.

Common spotted orchid (Dactylorhiza fuchsii)

Flowering time May–June.
Locations meadow areas.
See Walk June A.

Common spotted orchids are fabulous: ignore the word *common*. These, along with the other orchids, are what my eyes search for in the meadows and I'm frequently misled by a luscious specimen of red clover.

The tall (up to 30cm) spike is thick with flowers whose colours vary from white to lilac to pink, usually

minutely stencilled with cerise or purple. Leaves are dotted with purple. Sometimes I can detect a slight fragrance from the flower head.

Cowslip (*Primula veris*)

Flowering time	April–May.
Locations	lower part of Christ Church Green; meadows next to Circular Road; Durdham Down football areas; Zoo Banks. Can appear anywhere.
See Walk	April B.

Cowslips appear suddenly, or so it seems, with yet another shade of spring yellow – soft with a touch of lime. In the mown areas, especially the football pitches, the nodding flowers bloom on short stems because they have learned to flower quickly. Elsewhere they are up to 28cm tall carrying up to 25 flowers on one head. Leaves are wrinkled and toothed and form rosettes.

Significantly, these are companion flowers to green-winged orchids (*Orchis morio*) preferring the same conditions: in some years there are one of two of these orchids with cowslips on the Downs. We can hope for more –there are hundreds of cowslips and green-winged orchids growing together at Ashton Court.

Cowslips are referred to as *St Peter's Keys* in Somerset; this refers to their bunch of key appearance. *Cowslip* could be a reference to the flowers smelling like the breath of cows: Saxon *Cuslippe*. I think that the flowers smell like sherbet, although other botanists have detected the scent of aniseed and apricot.

Cuckoo flower (*Cardamine pratensis*)
otherwise widely known as **lady's smock**.

Flowering time	April–May.
Locations	Fairyland Glade; Granny Downs; Zoo Banks; in the area around the Water Tower.
See Walk	April A.

Cuckoo flower is a pretty flower that is increasing on the Downs but decreasing nationally. There are several explanations for its name – one is that it flowers when the cuckoo calls (although I last heard the cuckoo on the Bristol Downs on 8th May 1991). Another explanation, from the sixteenth century, is that the flower is often covered in cuckoo-spit, the foamy substance produced by the frog-hopper nymph.

Shakespeare uses an older name:

> *Daisies pied and violets blue,*
> *And lady-smocks all silver white.*
> (Loves Labours Lost Vii 894–896)

This may refer to ladies' linen laid out on the grass to dry, and bleached by the sun. Or possibly the linen uniforms worn by maids.

Each flower has four petals and is a delicate pale lilac or pink, veined with a darker shade. Sometimes the flowers seem white until put on a white sheet of a notebook for comparison. The leaves are dark green and taste like watercress.

Cuckoo-pint (*Arum maculatum*) widely known as **Lords and ladies**.

Flowering time	leaves and spathe: January–March. Flowers April–May. Berries August–September.
Locations	under bushes all over the Downs, especially Circular Road; Fairyland; The Promenade; Observatory Hill.
See Walk	Feb A, April B, Aug B.

Cuckoo-pint is an entertaining plant in its hooded, flower and berry stages. Large arrow-shaped leaves (plain or splotched with purple) appear from late January. The rather sinister hood (*spathe*) wrapped around the flower-head appears a few weeks later, and clumps of these resemble the ku klux klan. The flower head itself is a cylindrical rod, around 8cm long (this varies) and called a *spadix*.

The *spadix* is warm and smelly, encouraging flies to land on it and pollinate the plant. Moreover, the *spadix* can be purple, green or yellow. Purple is the most frequent on the Downs, and nationally.

There's coarseness about the plant, but for a day or two, when the hood is freshly unfurled and the sun shining onto the purple or yellow *spadix*, cuckoo-pint is as lovely as any other lily.

Pollinated flowers become scarlet or orange berries on a stalk up to 28cm high and are highly poisonous except to birds. I find them a welcome touch of colour in the early Autumn.

Folk names: *Lords-and-Ladies, Wake Robin, Cows-and-calves, and Friar's cowl.*

Dropwort (*Filipendula vulgaris*)

Flowering time late June–August.
Locations Zoo banks; Circular Road meadow.
See Walk July A.

Dropwort is too earthbound a name for these frothy, honey-scented, cream blossoms with sparkling yellow anthers and buds like coral beads. This flower is prized by chalk grassland nature reserves, and we have a fair showing here. It's easy to spot in the meadows as it grows to about 45cm.

In common with its close relative *meadowsweet*, dropwort was once used to treat kidney problems – possibly dropsy – hence the name.

Harebell (*Campanula rotundifolia*)

Flowering time July–October.
Locations Circular Road meadow; Clifton Down turf; Dumps; Zoo Banks.
See Walk Aug A.

Harebells with their simple, uplifting beauty follow the necessary mowing of our meadows: their translucence is that of blue butterflies or tiny fragments of the sky.

The bells bounce in the wind on wiry stems, 15 to 35cm high, and their local names are linked with magic: *witches' thimbles and fairy bells*. Folklore has it that the bells rang to warn hares of danger. I do not believe that hares have been recorded on the Downs, however.

Lady's bedstraw (*Galium verum*)

Flowering time	late June–September.
Locations	The Dumps; Zoo banks; all the meadows.
See Walk	July A.

Lady's bedstraw is a mid-summer delight. Masses of tiny yellow cut-grass scented flowers bloom on long square stems (up to 35cm) with slender, dark-green leaf whorls.

Mediaeval legend has it that Mary lay on a bed of this flower in Bethlehem because the donkeys had eaten all the other fodder; hence the flower's name.

The flowers were used to coagulate milk in cheese making – and to colour Double Gloucester cheese!

On the Downs, Lady's bedstraw keeps company with rock-roses, bird's-foot-trefoil, orchids, thyme, and later, tormentil and harebells.

Lesser celandine (*Ranunculus ficaria*)

Flowering time	February–April.
Locations	Along Saville Road; throughout the Granny Downs; Fairyland Glade; Observatory Hill.
See Walk	April A, April B.

Lesser celandines appear as a galaxy of yellow stars opening in the sun. The 16th century herbalist William Turner noted celandines *groweth under the shadowes of ash trees*. On the Downs they are more sociable, huddling under beech, horse chestnut, sycamore, and next to bluebells, speedwell, goosegrass, daisies, cowslips, dog's mercury, cuckoo flower, violets and nettles.

Celandine petals shine, an enamelling they share on the Downs with buttercups, and with the silverweed that grows around the dewpond on the Granny Downs.

Glossy, heart-shaped leaves appear in January and are often patterned with lighter green or bronze. Celandines flower on long stems (6–12cm) with 8–12 petals. Near Wills Hall, I once found a fasciated celandine 15cm high, its flower 5.2cm across: several flowers were fused together and there were so many petals that the flower could not close at night.

Lesser celandines grow throughout Northern Europe and are even been recorded near Moscow.

Ox eye daisy (*Leucanthemum vulgare*)

Flowering time	June–August.
Locations	White Tree meadow and the meadow areas around the Circular Road; Observatory Hill.
See Walk	June A.

Ox eye daisies are among the stars of the Downs' meadows. They are especially lovely when there are ox eye daisy buds as well as the flowers – points of laundry-fresh white in the grassy oceans. Buds and flowers lean towards the sun.

The flower heads are solitary, having an outer ring of white petals surrounding a core of gold. The stems can be up to 40cm high, and the flowers themselves up to 5cm in diameter. Leaves are long with zigzag edges.

Another, more romantic name is *Moon Daisy*, and in the Middle Ages, if a knight wore two daisies, he was the ladies' choice. Less romantic is the effectiveness of the plant as a flea deterrent.

Red valerian (*Centranthus ruber*)

Flowering time	April–September.
Locations	Avon Gorge rocks; Sea Walls; Observatory Hill.
See Walk	Aug A.

Red valerian is an attractive feature of the edge of the Avon Gorge. The roots bury themselves in crevices and even though the plant's height can reach 40cm, it is able to cling to rocks in high winds.

Red valerian was introduced from the Mediterranean in the 16th century as a garden plant, and it escaped and naturalised.

The honey-scented flowers can be pink, red, and white. Butterflies love them and I've seen painted lady, tortoiseshell and red admiral butterflies on them. Moreover in September 2006, I saw a hummingbird hawk moth on red valerian near the Peregrine Watch Point.

Young leaves can be eaten in salads.

Salad burnet (*Sanguisorba minor*)

Flowering time	May to August.
Locations	Zoo Banks and woods; Meadow Areas around Downs.
See Walk	June B.

Salad burnet is responsible for the fresh cucumber scent arising as we walk across meadow grass on the Downs. The strange flower usually escapes notice in favour of its brighter meadow companions, especially bird's-foot-trefoil, ox eye daisies and orchids.

The petal-less flowers occur on round heads bearing exquisite tufts of carmine red, and the lower part having from 30 to 40 stamens. When the stamens expand, long filaments hang around the head like golden tassels.

The flower-stem can be up to 30cm high and the dainty sprays of leaflets around the base are tasty in salads: hence the plant's name.

Small scabious (*Scabiosa columbaria*)

Flowering time	late June to September.
Locations	Downs' meadows; Zoo Banks; Clifton Down turf; Dumps; Observatory Hill.
See Walk	July A.

Small scabious is a refreshing touch of lilac-blue in the mid-summer meadows. The plant is about 30cm high and the flower heads are pretty pin-cushions 20–33mm across. These flowers are a very important nectar source for insects and give us opportunities to spot butterflies, bees and burnet moths.

The botanical name *scabious* comes from a Latin word-meaning *itch*, and the plant has been used to treat skin conditions. More romantically, the second part of the name *columbaria* is derived from the Latin for dove, or pigeon. This could refer to the divided leaves, or may indicate the pearly dove-lilac of the flower.

Spring cinquefoil (*Potentilla neumanniana*)

Flowering time	March–April.
Locations	Top of the Zoo Banks around rocks and in other grass at top of Fountain Hill; Observatory Hill.
See Walk	April A.

Spring cinquefoil – one of the Downs' rarities and my favourite for the startling citrus of its five notched petals. Its flowers are about 12mm in diameter on a short, trailing stem and the yellow is matt, not shiny like celandines. Spring cinquefoil is one of the Rose family and a close relation of the strawberry. In fact, the tiny dark green leaves resemble those of strawberry.

Sweet violet (*Viola odorata*)

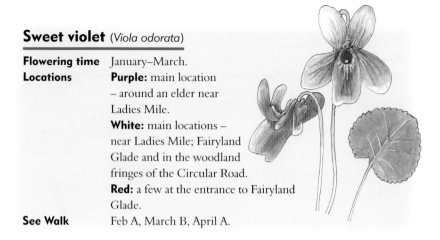

Flowering time	January–March.
Locations	**Purple:** main location – around an elder near Ladies Mile. **White:** main locations – near Ladies Mile; Fairyland Glade and in the woodland fringes of the Circular Road. **Red:** a few at the entrance to Fairyland Glade.
See Walk	Feb A, March B, April A.

Purple sweet violets bloom at the edge of winter in January with a perfume drawn, it seems to me, from the sweet fungal decay of autumn. Just one flower broadcasts its scent a long way and I found the largest patch near Ladies Mile by the fragrance, carried on a damp wind across fifteen metres. The heart-shaped leaves are scented, as are the seeds. The scent itself is lost the moment we enjoy it: sweet violets produce the chemical ionine, which temporarily dulls our sense of smell.

White sweet violets bloom from late February. The scent varies– the Downs' purple violets are the strongest, white gentler, and red is fresh with hints of rain and grass.

Red sweet violets, although rare, grow in abundance on the hillside of the Summerhouse Plantation, above the Mansion at Ashton Court. They're a deep cerise, fading rapidly in the sun to a dull rose red. On the Downs, a few flower in Fairyland.

Common dog-violets (*Viola riviniana*) begin to flower on the Downs in March, often in the open grass. These are unscented (hence the name *dog violets* – dog implying useless or inferior), and have longer stems than the sweet violet. One of the folk names for dog violets is *blue mice*. Dog violets have a long flowering season and I have often found single specimens in Fairyland in June.

Thyme *(Thymus polytrichus)*

Flowering time June–September.
Locations Downs' meadows; Dumps;
Zoo Banks; Observatory Hill.
See Walk June A.

Thyme – the favourite, fragrant flower of the fairies, and I'm minded of Shakespeare's

I know a bank where the wild thyme blows,
Where oxlips and the nodding violet grows …

On the Downs, thyme's short stems form purple cushions embroidered with clover, bird's-foot-trefoil, tormentil, butterflies and bumble bees. A widely used herb, the leaves contain thymol, an aromatic oil known to preserve and heal, supposedly a cure for toothache and nightmares.

Tormentil *(Potentilla erecta)*

Flowering time July–October.
Locations Circular Road meadow:
turf on Clifton Down.
See Walk Aug A.

Tormentil is scattered across Clifton Down turf like tiny golden buttons. The flowers (one cm across) have four petals and the upper leaves have the classic cinquefoil shape.

Tormentil is a member of the Rose family and is still highly prized for its medicinal and pain relieving properties, the name coming from the Latin *tormentum*.

On the Downs, they are an important source of nectar for solitary bees.

Yellow rattle (Rhinanthus minor)

Flowering time May–August.
Locations In the meadow areas,
especially above Zoo Banks.
See Walk June B.

Yellow rattle is increasing on the
Downs: it's cheerful and funny. Like its
companions, bird's-foot-trefoil and rock-
rose, yellow rattle grows in nice,
sunny spots: it's a plant of traditional
hay meadows and is also known as *hay
rattle*. It's a semi-parasite, getting minerals and water
by fixing on to the root system of grass next to it.

The bracts underneath the flower look like leaves,
and the golden petal tube (about 12mm in length)
resembles a witch's nose, giving rise to the plant's name
Rhinanthus coming from two Greek words meaning *nose*,
and *flower*. Adding to the witchy look are two purple or white teeth at the
tip of the tube.

The leaves are triangular, have rounded teeth and the plant is about
12–17cm high.

Another name for yellow rattle is *Rattle-box* – because the ripe seeds
rattle inside the pod. They were once given to babies to play with as their
mothers helped collect the hay crop. On the Downs, I've heard a patch
of these rattling pleasantly in the wind, and once, when I picked a stalk to
rattle it, a ladybird crawled out of the pod.

Rarities

Bristol whitebeam (*Sorbus bristoliensis*)
and Wilmott's whitebeam (*Sorbus wilmottiana*)

Flowering time   Creamy white flowers produced at the end
of May–early June.

Wilmott's whitebeam and Bristol whitebeam are two species of tree that
are endemic to the Avon Gorge (ie they grow wild here and nowhere else
in the rest of the world).

Bristol onion or
round-headed leek (*Allium sphaerocephalon*)

Flowering time   Magenta coloured flowers appear July–August.
Status   Red Data Book species. Nationally rare. The Avon
Gorge is the only place where this plant grows wild
in the UK.

Gardeners know these plants as 'drumsticks' as they produce a distinctive
ball of magenta flowers on a tall stem. The *sphaerocephalon* part of this
plant's scientific name means round-headed.

Bristol rock-cress (*Arabis scabra*)

Flowering time   Pink-tinged white flowers appear March – April.
Status   Red Data Book species. Nationally rare. The
Avon Gorge is the only place where this plant
grows in the UK.

For most of the year this plant consists of a rosette of dark
green leaves. The surface of their leaves are covered with small
hairs. *Scabra* means 'bristled'.

Western spiked speedwell (Veronica spicata ssp hybrida)

Flowering time   Purplish-blue flowers appear June–October.
Status   Nationally scarce.

This beautiful plant grows all over the limestone cliffs of St.
Vincent's rocks. In fruit, it resembles spent-sparklers, and is a
favourite food for voles and wood mice. Its first record in the UK was
here in 1634, but has probably grown on the cliff for thousands of years.

Autumn squill (Scilla autumnalis)

Flowering time   Mauve flowers appear July–September.
Status   Nationally scarce.

Before Brunel started to build this side of the Clifton Suspension
Bridge he had these rare plants dug up and re-planted further down
the Avon Gorge so that they didn't get destroyed during the construction.
    The *autumnalis* part of its name refers to its late flowering season.

Dwarf mouse-ear (Cerastium pumilum)

Flowering time   White flowers appear April–May.
Status   Nationally scarce.

This plant is so named because it's tiny and it has the most
delightful little mouse-ear shaped soft, hairy leaves.

Nit grass (Gastridium ventricosum)

Flowering time   June–August
Status   Red data book. Nationally rare.

The lime green flowering head or inflorescence of this very sweet
grass is covered in pale yellow blobs. From a distance it looks like it's
crawling with headlice or nits, hence the name.

Butterflies

Butterflies surprise us with sudden, jewelled colour – it's like finding treasure in the grass. Butterflies are often territorial and will return to the same rock, flower or leaf. Waiting for them to reappear is more rewarding than stalking them. If we want get close we must move as though in slow motion, soundlessly, and keep our shadows off them.

Brimstone (*Gonepteryx rhamni*)

Description **male** – upperside sulphur yellow with orange spot in middle of each wing. Underside duller and spots are brown. Wing shape is leaf-like and unique among British butterflies. **Females** – pale green yellow and often mistaken for large whites.

Life cycle one generation a year. Overwinters as a butterfly.

Caterpillar food plant on Downs Buckthorn.

Locations can be seen almost anywhere on Downs, especially around shrub islands and on Dumps. Often seen around areas of dog violets, and the few primroses on the Zoo banks.

Brimstone butterflies patrol territories and their journeys are predictable. They are powerful fliers and usually the first butterfly of the year, often patrolling the Dumps in February.

The peak time to see them is from the end of March to the middle of May, and then from the middle of August to the end of September. The adults hibernate in sheds and hollow trees, and when they fly in the early spring, I've noticed that they often rest in the shelter of brambles.

The vibrant yellow of this butterfly could be the origin of the word *butterfly* – contracted from *butter-coloured fly*. Unlike most other butterflies, the brimstone rests with closed wings so we need to spot it in flight to see the depth of colour of its upper wings.

Comma (*Polygonia c-album*)

Description uniquely jagged
wings. Upper side,
warm orange brown with
black and ochre markings.
underside, shades of bronze and
brown and in centre of hind wing
– a white comma-shaped marking, giving it the name. Females
are larger than males, and underside darker.

Life cycle two generations a year. Butterfly; April – November. Overwinters
as a butterfly.

Caterpillar food plant on Downs stinging nettle, elm, hazel.

Locations all meadow areas: Dumps; Zoo Banks; edges of Ash Wood and
Fairyland.

The comma surprises with its ornately sculptured wing edges, and
leaf-like camouflage when the wings are closed. The caterpillar is similarly
cryptic, resembling a bird dropping.

In the early twentieth century, the comma population mysteriously
crashed and was reduced to one or two sightings. By 1930, the population
began to recover and now the comma is familiar to those of us who walk
the Downs.

The size, warmth of colour, and the nature of the wing edges vary: the
butterfly can seem sun-faded, and the edges appear ragged to the point of
bird-pecked.

On the Downs, I see this butterfly on buddleia, hemp agrimony,
dandelions and blackberries.

Common blue (*Polyommatus icarus*)

Description **male** – upperside bright blue
with white fringes. Underside
grey-blue with white-ringed
black spots and orange markings
near margin.

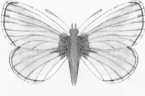

Female – upperside brown. Forewing has orange and black markings near margin – and a blue irridescence; hindwing has row of black spots edged with white and orange. Underside similar to male but on brown rather than blue-grey.

Life cycle   two generations a year, May to September.

Caterpillar food plants on Downs   bird's-foot-trefoil, black medick.

Locations   Dumps; Zoo Banks; Meadow areas.

The common blue butterfly is not now as prolific as its name suggests, and the shade of blue varies from sky to harebell, or even light violet. The Victorians were fascinated by fortuitous natural colour combinations and for me, the essence of summer is this butterfly on the yellow of bird's-foot-trefoil: the sky and the sun.

The common blue is highly active in the sunshine. When the weather is dull, wet or cold, it rests, wings closed and head down, on the flower stems of tall grasses in the meadow areas.

Holly blue (*Celastrina argiolus*)

Description   **male** upper side – deep sky blue. Black edging around wings. Fringes of forewings are white, chequered with black, fringes of hindwings are white. Underside pale blue with black spots. **Female** same blue as male but with broad black/brown borders. Underside is similar to male.

Life cycle   two generations a year. Butterfly – March – May, August – October. Overwinters as a pupa.

Caterpillar food plants on Downs   holly in spring, ivy in winter; also spindle and bramble.

Locations   Fairyland; Zoo banks; Ash Wood; Observatory Hill area.

The holly blue's upper wings are a rich azure, although this can be hard to see because the butterfly rarely opens its wings when resting.

These butterflies are tiny, and are sometimes mistaken for the common blue, although their shades of blue and locations are quite different. The common blue is the paler sky-blue and visits grasses and flowers, while the holly blue flies around bushes and trees. Moreover, the holly blue is in flight first.

The Downs is an ideal habitat for the holly blue butterfly. Its larval food plants are the holly in spring, and the ivy in the late summer. Spindle is also a food plant, and the Zoo Banks and Fairyland have plenty of this.

Although we rarely see the deep blue of the upper wings, the undersides are a unique silver-blue, especially noticeable against dark holly leaves.

Marbled white (*Melanargia galathea*)

Description	**male** – black markings on white. Underside markings paler. **Females** are larger and have brown markings on underside.
Life cycle	one generation a year –June to August. Over-winters as a caterpillar.
Caterpillar food plant on Downs	grasses, including cock's foot and sheep's fescue.
Locations	all meadow areas: Dumps.

The marbled white is uniquely coloured among British butterflies and is an optical illusion. It's a black butterfly with white markings (though I see it as a white butterfly with black markings) and a member of the *Satyridae* – the family of brown butterflies that includes the speckled wood and the meadow brown.

Marbled white butterflies return to the same flowers, favouring thistles, knapweed and small scabious. When it's cold and wet, they cling half way down grass stems, wings closed. Normally, it's hard to observe these butterflies closely as they are sensitive to proximity. There's a high-handed elegance in way the female scatters eggs in the grass during her flights in July and August. However, the lifespan of these magnificent butterflies is a mere one or two weeks.

Meadow brown (*Maniola jurtina*)

Description   **male** upper sides – dark brown with a black eye spot with white pupil set in little orange patch on forewing. Underside of forewing is mainly orange with an eyespot. Underside of the hindwings are brown with grey panel along the margin of the side. **Females** are larger and paler brown. The orange patch on the forewing is larger and they also have orange on the hindwing.

Life Cycle   one generation a year. Butterfly late June to September. Overwinters as caterpillar.

Caterpillar food plant on Downs   grasses.

Locations   all meadow areas on Downs and Zoo banks.

The meadow brown may be our most frequent butterfly. I love the way these butterflies fly up, a dozen or so at a time, as I walk through the long grasses. The intensity of the orange patches varies, and sometimes the whole butterfly can look faded. I've noticed that these butterflies do not fly very far, but stay within small areas of meadow grass. They will, however, fly when the sun is not shining.

Orange-tip (*Anthocharis cardamines*)

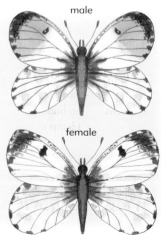

male

female

Description   **male** – upper side white. Forewing tipped with black, one black spot. Outer half of wing is orange. Underside, orange patch paler, tips of forewings and hind side mottled yellow and green. **Females** – large black spot on upper side and lack the orange patch. Underside, similar to males but lack orange.

Life cycle   one generation a year; April – June. Overwinters as pupa.
Caterpillar food plant on Downs   garlic mustard, cuckoo flower.
Locations   woodland edges in Dumps; Granny Downs; Zoo Banks, Fairyland.

The orange-tip butterfly is traditionally regarded as a herald of spring along with the cuckoo: I link its fruity colour with early summer. The orange may warn birds that the butterflies contain toxins from the larval food plants: certainly the male is more active and therefore more vulnerable to attack than the female.

The mottled undersides of this butterfly are an ideal camouflage when they are resting with closed wings.

On the Downs, I've seen the orange-tip butterfly on hawthorn, dandelion, cuckoo flower, garlic mustard, cow parsley, bluebell, and once, unexpectedly, on a sweet violet.

Peacock (*Inachis io*)

Description   upper wings are rust-red with large eyes in colours that resemble the feathers of a peacock. Under-wings are almost black with tracings of black lines, resembling tree bark. Sexes similar, female slightly larger.
Life Cycle   one generation a year. Overwinters as a butterfly, hibernating in hollow trees and rock crevices. In flight from March to October and can also be seen all year round when the temperatures are high enough.
Caterpillar food plant on Downs   stinging nettles (mainly in Dumps, Fairyland and Zoo Banks).
Locations   on buddleia on Granny Downs, Fairyland and near Ladies Mile. Hemp agrimony beside Circular Road, above Black Rock Gully.

Peacock butterflies surprise us by their magnificence, and by their presence on the Downs so early in the year. Adult peacock butterflies are amongst the first to be seen in the spring and I've observed one feeding on a bluebell near Fairyland. The 'eyes' may give predating birds the illusion that the butterfly is a larger creature than it is, and I have seen a blue tit hesitate to attack as a peacock flapped its wings with the sound of rustling leaves. These butterflies can live for up to eleven months.

Red admiral (Vanessa atalanta)

Description male and female alike, females slightly larger. Upper surface has black background. Forewing has scarlet band, white patches near tip, and electric blue on margins. Hindwing has marginal scarlet band containing black dots. Under side – forewings are similar but bluer. Hindwings are mottled with bronze, brown and black.

Life Cycle one or two generations a year. Flight time – March to November. A few overwinter as a butterfly, sometimes appearing as early as January. The red admiral can be seen all year round when the temperatures are high enough. Also migrant species from Europe.

Caterpillar food plant on Downs   nettles.

Locations Granny Downs; Fairyland Glade; Ladies Mile; Clifton Down; Dumps; Zoo Banks; Observatory Hill.

The red admiral is easy to study at close quarters. It feeds intensely and seems unconcerned by human proximity. We can observe this butterfly as it feeds on buddleia near Ladies Mile, on the Granny Downs and in Fairyland Glade. We can also see it throughout autumn, feasting on the widespread ivy flowers. The red admiral is a robust flyer, recorded flying at night and in extreme cold. I once saw it flying with its characteristic gliding flight, silhouetted against the rising sun, early on a cold September morning.

The name of this butterfly is not a naval reference (I assumed it was an allusion to its flag like appearance), but is believed to be a corruption of the 19th century name Red Admirable.

Small copper (Lycaena phlaeas)

Description male and female similar, female larger, duller and more rounded forewings. Upperside of forewings copper with small black spots and black marginal border. Hindwing black with wavy copper band next to hind margin. Underside of forewings coppery with small black spots. Hindwing pale brown with black dots.

Life cycle three generations a year, Mid April – mid July, and July – October. Overwinters as caterpillar.

Caterpillar food plant on Downs sorrel.

Locations Dumps; Zoo Banks.

The small copper butterfly is such a vibrant orange that it's easy to spot when settled. However, it is fast and tricky to watch in flight. The male is territorial and often returns to the same rock, stone or flower. I've seen this butterfly on bramble flowers, harebells and small scabious, and sunning on a rock on the Zoo Banks.

Small tortoiseshell (Aglais urticae)

Description upper side – ground colour is orange, with patches of black, yellow and white. Margins of fore and hind wings have blue markings. Underside brownish-black, with gold on the forewing. Sexes similar – females slightly larger.

Life cycle two generations a year: it is a butterfly for all months except part of June and part of August. Overwinters as a butterfly. Numbers may be diminishing.

Caterpillar food plant on Downs nettle (mainly in Dumps, Zoo Banks and Fairyland).

Locations on buddleia on Granny Downs, Clifton Down and Fairyland. On flowers in meadow grass areas, especially on thyme and scabious, and on red valerian around the Gorge areas.

The small tortoiseshell is a beautifully patterned, warmly coloured butterfly. It's fairy-like in flight, and has a tendency to open and close its wings quickly when disturbed. First individuals emerge from hibernation during late February and March and, along with the Brimstone and Peacock, surprise us by their presence so early in spring.

These butterflies often vary in size and colour, and certainly, I have noticed a difference in the warmth of the background colour. The pattern on the underside of the wings is thought to look like the shell of a tortoise. As a child, I wondered why fragments of small tortoiseshell wings were caught in spiders' webs: spiders are their major predator.

The speckled wood (Pararge aegeria)

Description	upper surface dark brown with pale yellow spots, some of which contain eye-spots. Underside lighter brown. Males smaller and darker than females with more pointed wings.
Life cycle	two generations a year, April to mid-October. Overwinters as either young caterpillar or pupae.
Caterpillar food plant on Downs	grasses such as cock's foot and couch.
Locations	all woodland edges including Granny Downs; Ash Wood; Fairyland, Circular Road Woods; Promenade Woods; Observatory Hill.

The speckled wood embodies the partially shaded landscape it favours: open-winged, it looks as though tiny points of sunlight are touching it through the leaves. I've often seen this butterfly making its way along the Granny Downs' footpath, and turning off to settle on a sun-dappled ash leaf.

Some males defend their territories, perching in a patch of sunlight and immediately rising to intercept intruders. I've frequently observed two of them in combat, spiralling up to the canopy, spot-lit by sun in Fairyland and the Ash Wood.

Speckled wood butterflies feed on the honeydew secreted by aphids.

Fungi

Fungi are the comedians of the wild: they entertain us with their inventiveness and cheek. They are also nature's composters, breaking down dead and dying matter to enrich the soil. Some fungi live in the roots of trees, and wildflowers such as bee orchids. Without their fungal partner, some trees and plants simply could not grow.

As for whether or not they are edible, I advise not. As the saying goes: *all fungi are edible, but some only once.* And while we may feel a mischievous urge to step on fungi, it's best to treat them like wild flowers and leave them for others to enjoy.

Earth star (*Geastrum fimbriatum*)

Fruiting body	star like – 2–3cm, 5–8 pointed rays. Cream. Raised central spore sack.
Found	under deciduous trees, in rich leaf-litter. Often solitary, but in small groups if we are lucky. Possible to find old specimens close to new ones.
Time of year	autumn, early spring.
On Downs	Fairyland; Zoo Banks.

Earth stars are romantic fungi, looking like fallen stars. They aren't common so I'm always proud of myself for finding them. The spore sacks are like miniature volcanoes and it's satisfying to gently press them to release a puff of brown spores: usually, the fungi depend on rain hitting the spore sack to do this.

Although earth stars can be elusive, there are many puffballs in the Downs' grassland, the meadow areas and the Zoo Banks. These are easy to find and offer the same puffing satisfaction.

Fairies' bonnets (*Coprinus disseminatus*)
also known as **Fairy inkcap** and **Trooping crumble cap**

Fruiting body	each bonnet is 0.5–1.5cm high, bell or thimble shaped. Pale buff or cream, deeply grooved and very fragile.
Found	On stumps of broad-leaved trees – massed groups of hundreds. Spread to nearby soil.
Time of year	late spring to late autumn.
On Downs	Granny Downs; Zoo Banks.

Fairies' bonnets are an enchanting world in miniature: they're short-lived and have thin, fragile stems. One June, I encountered a crowd of them by a horse chestnut on the Granny Downs, near the White Tree roundabout. I counted four hundred and eleven and missed several buses by doing so.

Jelly ear fungus (*Auricularia auricula-judae*)
also known as **Wood ear**

Fruiting body	3–8cm, shaped like an ear. Jelly texture, light brown exterior, velvet to the touch. Inner surface smooth and grey-brown; sometimes wrinkled. Becomes rubbery, then hard and blackens. Grows in groups.
Found	most frequently on elder branches.
Time of year	all year on the Downs but commonly in autumn and early spring.
On Downs	On elder, especially dead branches.

Jelly ear fungus is bizarre. Full-grown specimens are the size, shape and texture of ears. The earlier name *Jew's Ear Fungus* was graphic but regrettable: it's believed to refer to the supposed hanging of Judas Iscariot on an elder tree, and the fungi was probably originally known as *Judas' Ear*.

When these fungi are fresh, and the sun is shining through them, the ears are translucent purple. I often see them brushed with frost.

King Alfred's cakes (*Daldinia concentrica*)
also known as *cramp ball, the coal fungus* and *carbon balls*.

Fruiting body	2–10cm across, hemisphere, brown becoming shiny black. Spores released through tiny openings on surface. Usually in groups.
Found	on dead wood, mainly ash. Old, dried out fruiting bodies often persist for years, alongside new ones.
Time of year	all year.
On Downs	Zoo Banks; Fairyland; Promenade Woods; Ash Wood; Circular Road Woods.

King Alfred's cakes are unusual fungi.
They are rock-hard black balls growing typically on the branches of a dead or dying ash. In the past, they were used to treat cramp, hence the name: *cramp ball*. The current popular name reflects their likeness to burned cakes and this links them with King Alfred! Legend has it that King Alfred (reigned 871–899) was once in exile, hiding incognito in the house of a cowherd. The wife was baking cakes (or bread) and asked Alfred to keep an eye on them. He was so engrossed in making arrows that he allowed them to burn and received a thorough telling-off.

Often, several balls combine into a strange black mess more like a blackened curry than a cake.

Lawyer's wig *(Coprinus comatus)*
also known as Shaggy inkcap and Shaggy mane

Fruiting body	cap 5–15cm high, white with beige/gold centre, cylindrical. Breaks up into large shaggy scales, tipped with brown. Often in large groups. Smells pleasant.
Found	in grass by roadsides, on recently disturbed soil.
Time of year	summer to autumn.
On Downs	near Wills Hall; Granny Downs; Ladies Mile.

Lawyer's wig is a distinguished fungus, as befits its common name, and its past use as ink: spores have been found in old documents. One October, I counted 63 of these in the grass on the Granny Downs, in all stages from egg-like beginnings to inky black slop.

Shaggy Parasol *(Lepiota rhacodes)*

Fruiting body	cap about 5–15cm across with angular scales giving torn, ragged appearance. Thick stem has double ring. Strong 'mushroom' smell.
Found	woods, often near conifers.
Time of year	summer to late autumn.
On Downs	wooded areas, often inside hollowed out shrub islands, or around them as fairy rings.

Shaggy Parasol fungus is extraordinary for the sheer size of the caps (I once found a giant cap 20cm across on the Granny Downs) and for growing in big, complete fairy rings. When I return to view the rings for a second time, I invariably find that several if not all of the fungi are flattened, kicked over. Alas, large fungi seem to attract this response.

Stag's horn fungus (*Xylaria hypoxylon*)
also known as *Candlesnuff fungus*

Fruiting body	1–6cm high, flattened antler shape, black stalks and the branches powdered white.
Found	dead wood, mainly of deciduous trees.
Time of year	all year.
On Downs	often on tree stumps – Fairyland; Zoo Banks; Circular Road Woods; Granny Downs; Promenade Woods.

Stag's horn fungus is fascinating. It often clusters on tree stumps and looks as though the stump is holding dozens of extinguished candles: a birthday cake of the woods. Moreover, the texture is deceptive: I expect it to crumble like the ash it resembles, but it's rubbery and tough.

Stinkhorn (*Phallus impudicus*)

Fruiting body	starts as egg shaped, covered with leaf-litter. Egg ruptures and white stalk-like structure grows 10–25cm high. The head is covered by mesh over which there is a coating of grey-olive stinking slime. This contains the spores.
Found	woodland areas, associated with rotting wood in soil. Singly or in small groups.
Time of year	summer to late autumn.
On Downs	Fairyland; Zoo Banks; Circular Road woods; Ash Wood; Promenade Woods.

Stinkhorn is widely regarded as disgusting. I recommend a robust approach, however, because this is an interesting fungus not a practical joke. Its rotting meat stench is responsible for the gassy smell that often permeates woodlands in the late summer. Flies are greatly attracted to the smell, the slime sticks to their legs and thus spore dispersal is assured.

Stinkhorn does have a moment of appeal, however: after flies have removed the slime, the head is a pink mesh of raised ridges and there is a certain charm in this.

Waxcaps: (Hygrocybe)

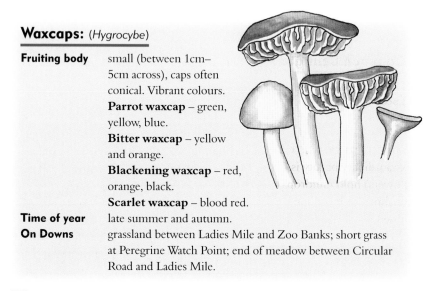

Fruiting body	small (between 1cm–5cm across), caps often conical. Vibrant colours. **Parrot waxcap** – green, yellow, blue. **Bitter waxcap** – yellow and orange. **Blackening waxcap** – red, orange, black. **Scarlet waxcap** – blood red.
Time of year	late summer and autumn.
On Downs	grassland between Ladies Mile and Zoo Banks; short grass at Peregrine Watch Point; end of meadow between Circular Road and Ladies Mile.

Waxcaps are surprising, a sudden shock of vivid colour – a dropped button? Treasure? Sometimes there's a fairy ring of waxcaps in the grass, or around a shrub. These fungi are translucent and their slimy caps gleam: they are the magic toadstools of our imagination, and we can envisage fairies living amongst them, or using them as umbrellas.

Waxcaps are one of the groups of fungi used to indicate how good a grassland is.

Grasses

Grasses are more than just the supporting cast in the wild picture. If the beauty of grasses is unknown to you, start with this tiny selection.

Common bent grass (*Agrostis capillaris*)

Flowering time June–August.
Locations Downs' meadows.
See walk July A, July B.

Common bent grass is widespread on the Downs and its extraordinary beauty is evident after rain – the purple spikelets (flowers) hold raindrops and they sparkle, diamonds in the sunshine. In fact, they hold so much rain that the misty patches shine like water, and lap around harebells like wind-ruffled puddles.

When it's not wet, common bent swirls its purple currents in the grassy oceans.

Common quaking grass (*Briza media*)

Flowering time May–August.
Locations Downs' meadow grasslands,
and Zoo Banks.
See walk June A, July B.

Common quaking grass rattles in the wind, but you may have to kneel beside it to hear this. The flower heads are loosely pyramidal and the spikelets (flowers) hang and tremble on hair-like stalks. The spikelets themselves are exquisitely enamelled in purple and green, and in the sun they shine like exotic beetles. The grass has sparse foliage, only a few pointed leaves.

Common quaking grass has many folk names: *rattle grass*, *totter grass*, *shivering grass*, *cow quakes*, *doddering dickies* and *didder*.

Upright brome (Bromopsis erecta)

Flowering time June–August.
Locations Downs' meadows.
See walk July B.

Upright brome is tall (40–120cm) and forms the crest of the waves in the Downs' meadows. It bends, sways and ripples with the wind. The spikelets (flowers) are usually purplish-brown. After rain, raindrops congregate along the stems, and when it's cold, wet, or at night, marbled white and meadow brown butterflies cling to them.

Children love to run through this grass with their arms bare so they can feel it.

Wood melick (Melica uniflora)

Flowering time May–July.
Locations Fairyland paths.
For walk Visit Fairyland in flowering season.

Wood melick is the most beautiful of the woodland grasses, and for me, very exciting because it is associated with ancient woodlands. In Fairyland, it's a companion grass to bluebells and dog's mercury – also signs of long-established woodlands.

The bright green blades of the grass form patches, and the flower heads are branched, but less intricately so than quaking grass which it superficially resembles.

The flower is egg shaped and called a *spikelet*. Pollinated by the wind, the seeds ripen and the enclosing scales become shiny and hard.

Trees and Shrubs

The trees of the Bristol Downs are its beloved living landmarks and this is my small selection of them.

Ash *(Fraxinus excelsior)*

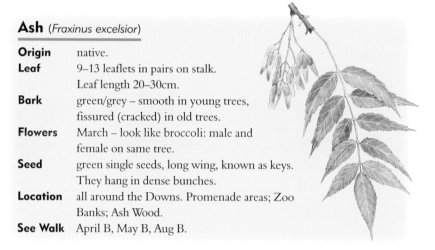

Origin	native.
Leaf	9–13 leaflets in pairs on stalk. Leaf length 20–30cm.
Bark	green/grey – smooth in young trees, fissured (cracked) in old trees.
Flowers	March – look like broccoli: male and female on same tree.
Seed	green single seeds, long wing, known as keys. They hang in dense bunches.
Location	all around the Downs. Promenade areas; Zoo Banks; Ash Wood.
See Walk	April B, May B, Aug B.

The ash of Norse mythology is sacred, touching and uniting heaven and hell. Here, an ash unites night and day when the branches of the giant ash on Clifton Down seem to touch the rising sun and the fading moon. Starlings collect in this landmark ash and the tree is alive with musical chatter. Small birds – goldfinches, great tits, long-tailed tits – weave around the branches: once I watched a brimstone butterfly rise to the top of the canopy.

Ash buds resemble fingernails dabbed with soot, and the ash is the last tree to come to full leaf in the spring. Sometimes bunches of ash keys remain on the tree, turn brown and hang down like rags.

Fresh ash keys are a favourite food of woodpigeons.

Beech (*Fagus sylvatica*)

Origin	native.
Leaf	6–9cm arising first on one side of the twig, then the other (alternate), glossy green on both surfaces. When held up to the light, or backlit by the sun, we can see the fine hairs at the edges of the leaves.
Bark	smooth grey.
Flowers	April – yellow male flowers hang like tassels on long stalks. Female flowers, greeny white.
Fruits	small nuts in four-valved husk. Nut cases woody and bristly.
Location	Durdham Down; The Promenade; the Avenue; the Granny Downs.
See Walk	Sept B, Oct B, Nov A.

The beeches on the Downs are formidable. It's exciting to see them toss their massive domes in high winds and to hear that ocean roar as the wind whips through the leaves.

The beech is the best tree to watch to note the changing seasons. At first, the leaves are the lightest of green and to hold them is like cradling air. After about a month, the leaves are thicker and darker and this coarsening continues throughout the year until the winter.

In the autumn, the leaves turn first yellow, then an orange brown. Young trees retain their leaves throughout the winter and they rustle like taffeta in the wind.

The nuts are small but tasty, and the empty cases are like wooden flowers, making striking table decorations.

Copper beeches give the Downs rich purple landmarks: they are exquisitely pink on sunny days in early spring, and an inspired inclusion in the Avenue of trees (once known as the Elm Ride).

Birch (silver) (*Betula pendula*)

Origin	native.
Leaf	oval, or triangular, about 2.5–4cm long, thin and shiny on slender stalks. Leaf edges are ragged. The base of the leaf is usually straight, although some are kite-shaped.
Bark	silvery white with black, diamond shaped patches, developing with age into rugged cracks near base of trunk.
Flowers	late March – yellow male catkins with spots of purple pollen, and pale green female catkins (on same tree).
Fruit	fruiting catkins remain on tree until winter, then break up into scales and tiny wind-borne seeds.
Locations	Granny Downs; Clifton Down; Circular Road; Behind Downs Tea Rooms: Zoo Banks near Fairyland; Christ Church Green.
See Walk	Nov A, Nov B.

The silver birch is delicately detailed, and carries its beauty modestly until the late autumn when it rivals the fireworks with its silver trunk and sparkling golden leaves.

In spite of its graceful, pliant appearance, the silver birch is one of the world's hardiest trees and it is native to Britain.

Pagan Celtic and Germanic tribes revered the tree as holy. It was considered to have powers of renewal and purification and its twigs were used in the ritual of driving out the spirits of the old year. This belief persisted into more modern times when delinquents were birched to drive out evil spirits.

The silver birch supports over two hundred varieties of insect.

Before new leaves appear in spring, twigs and buds appear dark red. New leaves are at first bright green, quickly darkening to a duller shade. During September and October, the leaves are a shimmering patchwork of yellow and green, and in late November/December the tree becomes fully golden.

The silver birch is known as *the lady of the woods* and I think it is the most beautiful of all trees in the moonlight.

Elder *(Sambucus nigra)*

Origin	native.
Leaf	5–7 toothed leaflets on stalks, arranged in pairs on the twigs.
Bark	grey-brown, thick and ridged.
Flowers	May onwards, creamy white. Hundreds of tiny flowers form flat, plate-like heads with strong, sweet scent.
Fruit	purple-black berries hang in bunches from late August.
Location	Clifton Down, especially the Dumps and Ladies Mile areas.
See Walk	June B, Aug B, Sept A.

The history of the elder is rich in alarming folklore warning of its malign influence. It was believed that Jesus was crucified on a cross of elder. Apparently no plant will grow in its shade and it has names such as *Devil's Eye*, *Tree of Doom*, *God's Stinking Tree*. Yet the elder is so useful, and was traditionally known as the *medicine chest of the people*.

The flowers and berries (rich in vitamin C) are widely used in winemaking and cookery: for a long time these were also incorporated in medicines and complexion enhancers.

As for *Stinking Tree*, elder flowers are better smelled on a breeze than at close quarters, but this is the case with hawthorn, wayfaring tree blossom, privet, horse chestnut spires and even violets.

An elder bower near Ladies Mile protects hundreds of winter-flowering purple sweet violets. In early spring, the dead branches of this same bower sport the realistic *jelly ear fungus*. And in the autumn, elders offer us opportunities to grin at the woodpigeons that perch on their slender branches and overreach themselves trying to grab the berries.

As a child, one of my missions was to find elderflower heads with tiny carmine flowers among the white: they gave me permission to make a wish. Some of these wishes came true, but in the manner of wishes, not immediately.

Hawthorn (*Crataegus monogyna*)

Origin	native.
Leaf	small (3–4cm) and deeply indented leaves arranged first on one side of a twig, then on the other.
Bark	browny-grey, fairly smooth, but rippled in older trees. Twigs are thorny.
Flowers	May – white, sometimes blushed with pink. Strong, sweet smell. There are varieties on the Downs with deep pink and double-petalled flowers.
Fruit	September onwards – fleshy, dark red fruits called haws, each one containing a single seed.
Locations	Granny Downs; Clifton Down; Ladies Mile area – particularly between Ladies Mile and Clifton Down Road.
See walk	May B, Aug B, Sept A, Sept B.

The hawthorn is the only tree to be named after the month in which it flowers. Our hawthorns are celebrated, and *going up the Downs to see the may* is a spring mission for many Bristol people.

The hawthorn has long been considered a sacred, healing tree: it's also the origin of the maypole, and the blossoms that were used in May Day decorations.

Hawthorn is traditionally the tree of the Fairy Queen. One spring custom was to make little crowns of hawthorn blossom and leave them out at night for the fairies. Supposedly, fairies can be seen where oak, ash and hawthorn grow together. The Granny Downs has all three, as has the area known as the Ranger's Pound, but possibly the trees are not close enough to each other.

The scent is best carried on a cool wind and is heady on a cold evening or a frosty morning. Warmth reveals a sickly-sweet aspect: hawthorn scent contains trimethylene that is also the scent of decay. Hawthorn is largely pollinated by dung flies and midges attracted by this smell.

It's widely considered unlucky to bring the blossom indoors, however much its beauty tempts us.

Hawthorns are important for wildlife: blackbirds and finches nest in them, and their berries feed many species of birds, notably the redwings that gather on the Granny Downs and around Ladies Mile. The trunks of older hawthorns are often twisted and knotty and this seems to enhance their beauty, especially when they are full of blossom or berries.

Hazel (*Corylus avellana*)

Origin	native.
Leaf	May – arranged on twigs first on one side, then the other (alternate) with saw-tooth edges; surfaces are soft and hairy.
Bark	light brown, scaly in older trees.
Flowers	February – male flowers – lime green/yellow catkins: female flowers are tiny buds with an intense red cone of stigmas 5mm across. The female flowers become the nuts.
Fruit	October – nuts grow in clusters, each nut held in green helmet of bracts (seed bearing structure).
Locations	Zoo Banks; Fairyland Glade; Woodlands near Peregrine Watch Point.
See walk	Jan A, Feb A, Feb B.

Hazel bushes on the Downs are not plentiful, but are worth seeking out.

Hazel catkins appear in the autumn. At first they are tightly packed and the bush looks as though green snow is falling through the branches. The male catkins open in February when little else is in leaf or flower, and awaken our anticipation of spring: their likeness to lambs' tails intensifies this.

When the catkins loosen and lengthen, they become a unique lemon-green: I can't resist tapping them to release pollen. Female flowers, on the same bush, are tiny brushes of vivid red and are sometimes hard to find.

Whether the catkins are tight or loose, this is the most beautiful bush in silhouette against the rising sun, a blue sky or a low moon. Birds of the tit family, and goldcrests, use the branches as playgrounds, hanging upside down on the swaying catkins as they search for hidden insects and spiders.

Hazel rods are prized for their pliancy and were used to build coracles, baskets and in house building. Magic wands were (and are) made of hazel wood, and forked hazel twigs are used in water divining.

The nuts are a favourite of mice, squirrels, jays and woodpigeons.

Horse chestnut (Aesculus hippocastanum)

Origin	brought here from Balkans in 16th Century.
Leaf	fragrant sticky buds open in spring to produce between five and seven large stalk-less leaflets. Looks like giant hand.
Bark	grey or ruddy brown. Scales in older trees.
Flowers	May – large white fragrant spikes – candles.
Fruit	conkers, enclosed in spiny green cases. Ripe mid-September onwards.
Location	Mainly Durdham Down; Granny Downs; Stoke Road, Westbury Road.
See Walk	April A, May A, Sept B, Oct A, Nov A.

Horse chestnuts are magnificent. These trees are the centre of attention in spring, when the avenues of blossoming trees are awesome; and in autumn when it's conker time and the fallen leaves are cloths of gold.

Children look for conkers from August onwards, but these are unripe and white. Conkers will fall when they are ready and then, the vibration of passing cars brings down several at once. For a while the conkers remain glossy, and comparing the watermark patterns on them, we can see that each conker is unique.

The trunks of horse chestnuts seem especially accommodating for climbing squirrels: some have deep, spiral grooves as though a giant hand had wrung them out.

Note: There are red chestnuts on Stoke Road and Westbury Road. These are a cross between common horse chestnut and red buckeye. Red chestnuts do not have sticky buds and their conker cases are spineless.

Limes include:

Small leaved *Tilia cordata*, **Common** *Tilia x europaea*, **Silver** *Tilia tomentosa*
Large-leaved or **broad-leaved** *Tilia platyphyllos*

From this abundance of limes, I'm featuring

Large-leaved Lime (Tilia platyphyllos)

Origin	native.
Leaf	arranged alternately along the twigs, large, heart-shaped, up to 15cm long. Dark green, hairy on top, paler and even hairier underneath.
Bark	smooth and grey with fine fissures (cracks).
Flowers	late June, green-yellow, hanging in clusters of three or four. Sweet smelling, attracting bees.
Fruits	hanging, felt-textured fruits, three or four in each cluster. These are the limes with the largest fruits on the Downs.
Locations	Granny Downs, and abundant along Ladies Mile. Also Circular Road; top end of Clifton Down.
See Walk	July A, Aug A, Sept B, Nov A.

Lime flowers are a mid-summer treat. Moreover, the flowers of the varieties of this tree open at slightly different times, and extend the experience throughout late June and July. The large-leaved lime flowers appear slightly earlier than the flowers of the other varieties, and there is a magnificent avenue of them across the Granny Downs. These are reckoned to be about 200 years old. The large-leaved lime is also interplanted with other lime species along Ladies Mile.

Limes were planted as long ago as Roman times for their glorious scent, and for their shade. The scent of the flowers is as uplifting close-to as it is carried on the breeze: in my experience, this is unusual.

The Japanese practise *shinrin-yoku* – wood-air bathing – for the healing and peace of mind that comes from breathing the air of woods. Walking in a linden-blossom breeze makes me feel optimistic, thankful and young again.

The winged seeds spiral down elegantly, and after germination the seed leaves are like little green hands, prising open the earth.

Oak (*Quercus robur*)

Origin	native. Oaks are known to have grown in Britain before the last Ice Age.
Leaf	arranged alternately on twigs, growing on very short stalks as opposed to those of sessile oaks that grow on long stalks. Four or five lobes on each side of the leaf.
Bark	smooth brown bark in young trees, grey-brown, furrowed vertically in old trees.
Flowers	May. Male flowers slender yellow catkins, female flowers tiny clusters resembling dark red bells at end of shoots.
Fruit	ripe from September – acorns – often in pairs on long stalks.
Locations	Circular Road Woods; Clifton Down; Ladies Mile area; Zoo Banks; The Promenade.
See walk	Aug B, Oct B.

The oak has majesty and tradition, yet it's a homely tree and an ideal picnic companion: sunlight beams prettily through its open canopy.

New oak leaves are uniquely bronze and this is one of my markers for the beginning of spring. Male flowers are light green catkins and I think that these, along with many tree flowers, escape notice because when they appear in May, there are so many wild flowers to see that we rarely look up.

In Celtic Britain, the oak was regarded as sacred and since then, the English oak has been called the King of British trees. The wood has been used in furniture, cathedrals and ships. The Royal Navy march *Hearts of Oak* has the chorus:

> *Hearts of oak are our ships,*
> *Jolly Tars are our men …*

Other versions of this have it that *hearts of oak are our men.*

It is between 40–50 years before an oak grows sufficiently to have a sizeable acorn crop of its own. Acorns – both green and later, shiny brown, are multi-textured works of art, the rough, patterned cup contrasting with the smooth acorn.

Oaks exhibit many galls: these are abnormal tissue growths produced by the plant as a result of chemicals secreted by the gall wasp. More than 30 species of gall wasps occur on the English oak. On Downs' oaks, I've seen oak apple gall, knopper gall, spangle gall, artichoke gall, marble and currant gall. These galls contain the grubs of the gall wasp and later in the year, bluetits and great tits seek them out to eat.

The English oak supports more species of wildlife than any other tree in Britain; the acorns feed squirrels, badgers, mice, jays and rooks; the tree supports nearly 300 varieties of insect, those in the bark encouraging great spotted woodpeckers. The dead leaves, rotted, form a rich leaf mould for worms and insects; and the dead wood of the tree supports fungi and insect grubs.

Other varieties of Oak on the Downs

Sessile oak (*Quercus petraea*) leaves 9–12cm, wedge-shaped leaf base, distinct leaf stalks. Acorns stubby and without stalks.

Turkey oak (*Quercus cerris*) leaves 8–13cm deeply lobed, dark green, shiny on top. Acorns in mossy cups. Tree late to lose leaves in autumn.

Holm oak (*Quercus ilex*) evergreen. Young leaves broad with spines, old, upper leaves narrow without teeth. Very dark green on top, lighter and hairy underneath. Pale green acorns, enclosed by scaly cups.

Spindle (*Euonymus europaeus*)

Origin	native.
Leaf	arranged in opposite pairs, 3–8cm long. Lance-shaped leaves turn red in autumn.
Bark	grey/green, smooth. Twigs often distinctly square.
Flowers	May–June – small, barely conspicuous yellow/green flowers. Four petals. Rich in nectar, attracting small pollinating insects such as hoverflies, bees and the dangly-legged St Mark's flies.
Fruits	ripen in September and October – four-lobed seed capsules, turning a matt powder pink or deep red when ripe. Four seeds contained within orange fleshy layer called aril. The berries are very poisonous.
Locations	Zoo Banks; Fairyland and near Peregrine Watch Point.
See Walk	Aug B, Sept A, Jan A.

Spindle is easy to overlook until the autumn when it demands attention. Then, the leaves turn to yellow, then scarlet, and clusters of pink seed capsules hang like lanterns.

As a child, I regarded this as a tree specially decorated for fairies, and the *Spindle Fairy* was my favourite of Cecily Mary Barker's *Flower Fairies of the Winter*. Her lines are the best description of its autumn colours:

> See the rosy-berried Spindle
> All to sunset colours turning

The fruit is highly poisonous to us: however, birds are attracted to the seeds, eat and disperse them with no ill effects. Its common name reflects its use for making wooden spindles used for spinning wool. The spindle is also known as *Prickwood, Skewerwood and Pincushion Shrub*.

The leaves of the spindle contain a toxin and were once dried and powdered to kill head lice.

Spindle is a food plant of the holly blue butterfly.

Sycamore (*Acer pseudoplatanus*)

Origin	not native to Britain, believed to have been introduced to Ireland around 15th–16th centuries. Native of Europe and Western Asia.
Leaf	arranged in pairs along the twigs, large, five-lobed leaves. Upper sides dark green.
Bark	grey and fissured (cracked).
Flowers	April – dense, hanging yellow flowers: 20–50 flowers on each stalk.
Fruit	June onwards, fertilised female flowers become paired seeds, each seed with a long (20–40mm) wing to catch the wind and rotate, taking the seed away from the parent tree.
Locations	Ladies Mile; Granny Downs; Observatory Hill; Christ Church Green; Promenade Woods; Zoo Banks.
See Walk	Sept A.

Sycamores are impressive trees with lovely details. Sycamores have an exquisite leaf unfolding sequence: the newly opened bud case is rosy brown, and the pleated leaves a vivid lime green. Sometimes the yellow flowers are flushed bronze pink. Later, the wings of the seeds are brushed with coral before they dry, ready to fall; and shades of pink sometimes return in the autumn leaves.

It's great to introduce children to the spiralling 'helicopter' seeds: we may need to demonstrate that it is single wings that fly, not the attached pair.

Squirrels eat the nuts as soon as they are formed and they leave the discarded wings on their *squirrel tables* – usually tree stumps and small rocks.

The flowers are an important source of nectar and pollen for bees: sycamore honey is very fragrant.

Wych elm (*Ulmus glabra*)

Origin	native.
Leaf	arranged alternately along the twigs, about 14cm long. Rather rough textured. Edge double-toothed. Green in spring, yellow in autumn.
Bark	grey with long fissures (cracks).
Flowers	February, before the leaves. Carmine pink, at first the flower buds are like tight rosebuds, developing into tufts of red flowers.
Fruits	July – papery circles with an orange/brown seed in the centre.
Location	Clifton and Durdham Down; Promenade woodlands; Ladies Mile.
See Walk	Oct B, Feb A.

Elms on the Downs are now largely represented by the wych elms: these are broader than English elms, but do not grow so high. English elms are actually evident on the Downs, but they always succumb to Dutch elm disease before they become 'tree' sized. There is a large area of these at the bottom of Ladies Mile.

Wych comes from an Anglo-Saxon word meaning *pliable*. The twigs are pliable and many horsemen carried riding-whips made from them.

The wych elm has moments of glory. The flower buds appear in February (before the leaves) and the tree has a deep pink aura around it, visible from a distance. It's magical to stand under the branches, looking up at the tracery of the canopy.

The leaves are at first a luminous pale green, and in autumn they are spectacularly yellow.

Note: Other elms occur on the Downs. The English elm (as a sucker). The "Sapporo autumn gold" on Christ Church Green: this is a hybrid between a Siberian and a Japanese elm, bred to be resistant to Dutch elm disease. It has a very distinctive herring bone arrangement of twigs along the branch.

63

Yew (*Taxus baccata*)

Origin	native.
Leaf	evergreen needles – dark, matt green.
Bark	thin, and flakes to reveal reddish-brown, smooth patches which are especially red when wet.
Flowers	yews are dioecious – they usually bear either male or female flowers. Male trees flower late in winter or early spring, producing small catkins with plentiful wind-borne pollen. Female flowers are tiny and bright green and only one seed is produced from each.
Fruit	grows on female trees throughout the summer and the single hard seed is partly embedded in a fleshy translucent red cup (aril) in September. The seeds take 18 months to germinate.
Locations	Clifton Down especially near Ladies Mile and the Circular Road. Outside the Downs Tea Rooms; Fairyland; Zoo Banks.
See Walk	Sept A, Feb A, Nov B.

Yews are glorious for their darkness, their permanence and their pollen and berries. These trees offer shelter from cold and rain, and I often stand beneath them listening to goldcrests searching for insects in the canopy above me.

Most trees' leaves rustle in the wind: the yew is quiet and I believe that I could walk under it blindfolded without being aware of its presence.

In the UK, yew is one of only three native conifers along with juniper and Scots pine. The tree is reputed to live longer than most other species that will grow in the United Kingdom and many are well over 1,000 years old.

In legend, the yew is a symbol of immortality and is widely planted in churchyards.

Yew berries are exquisite, especially in the sun or snow: they sometimes feature on Christmas cards. Equally remarkable are the clouds of pollen released when the mimosa-like male flowers are lightly tapped in February.

All parts of the yew are poisonous except the flesh of the fruit and this is beloved of birds, especially thrushes: the seed itself is poisonous.

Birds on the Bristol Downs

Watching birds on the Downs is fascinating because the birds are accustomed to living alongside us, and are less elusive and alarmist than their woodland counterparts. The Downs has a variety of tall trees, and many shrub islands – clumps of shrubs bound together by ivy – which are ideal cover for small birds.

Birds are loyal to their territories, trees, and shrub islands and so we can often predict what we will see. My family first learned the wildlife of the Downs by adopting a shrub island on the Zoo Banks, visiting it every week and seeing what happened.

Some shrub islands contain dead trees. It's fortunate that these dead branches remain because they are often the highest places and birds frequently perch on them, giving us a perfect view.

For those new to bird-watching, it may be helpful to know that:

- It's usually the male bird that sings: female birds make contact calls. Robins are an exception as both sexes sing.
- Bird song is about territory and attracting a mate so it's mainly heard in the spring months – February to May. It's also heard to a lesser extent in the autumn when birds are re-establishing their territories, and juveniles are establishing them for the first time.
- Peak time for birdsong is the early morning, and the evening.
- Female birds are generally less colourful than the male so that they are inconspicuous when on the nest. Juveniles, too, are often duller and not so vulnerable to predators.
- The Dawn Chorus occurs between the middle of March and May and can begin as early as four thirty in the morning

There are dozens of species of bird on the Downs and in the Gorge, living here all year, arriving in the spring to nest, over wintering, or passing through. Their number varies from year to year. This is my selection.

Blackbird (*Turdus merula*)

Status	resident, joined by migrants in winter.
Description	adult male (25cm) black with yellow/ orange bill and yellow ring around eye. Female warm brown and has fuzzy spots on throat and breast.
Food	worms, insects, fruit and berries. Recently reported in this area eating snails, like thrushes.
Nest	In low tree or hedge, solid cup of dried grass and twigs, lined with mud. Lays March–April, 3–5 eggs, hatch in two weeks. Can have three or four families throughout the year and there are reports of them nesting in December and January. Young fledged after 14 days but remain with parents for further three weeks.
Locations	Shrub islands all around Downs.

Blackbirds here are less alarmist than their cousins across the Gorge: In Leigh Woods they are elusive, woodland birds.

Early in the morning, male blackbirds sit by shrubs, and then perch higher up when the light increases. The blackbird's song is commanding and fluty. They also utter a jangling *chink chink* to keep others away from their roosting sites, and for several weeks each year, this begins at half past four on the Granny Downs.

Partial albino blackbirds are sometimes seen here, and recently, I watched a bald blackbird sing from the top of a hawthorn. He had no neck or head feathers and it was as though his skull was singing. However, he lived for at least two months after that, and I last saw him with a female blackbird.

During small flurries of snow in winter, blackbirds leap up to catch the flakes like insects: I have also seen them jump up to catch raindrops in this way.

Blackcap (Sylvia atricapilla)

Status	visitor – late March–October: some birds from Germany and north-east Europe over winter here, mainly in South-West and often on Bristol Downs.
Description	a warbler with a grey body and brown wings, about 13cm. Male has jet-black cap, females and young birds a chestnut brown cap.
Food	caterpillars and other insects; berries, especially ivy and elder, and tree flowers.
Nest	Wooded fringes, deep in briars, shrubs and bushes. Flimsy cups, lined with grass. The male often builds several nests and the female chooses one of them. Lays May–July (two broods) 4–5 eggs, hatch in about 12–14 days.
Locations	Wooded fringes; shrub islands; Fairyland; Dumps; Zoo banks; Ash Wood; Observatory Hill.

The blackcap is often first heard amongst the blossom of the Downs – the blackthorn around the Circular Road, and later the hawthorn. Blackcaps sing from cover with a song so clear and vibrant that it sounds as though it's broadcast from the treetops.

The song is a waterfall of notes, fast and bubbling: blackcaps are sometimes referred to as *mock nightingales* or *northern nightingales*. Blackcaps will stop singing if we walk too close and resume singing when we are sufficiently past. They also utter a sharp *tak tak* alarm call that sounds like two rocks being knocked together.

Black-headed gull (Larus ridibundus)

Status	late summer to winter visitor.
Description	36–38cm. In breeding season, adult has pale grey wings and white body with a chocolate brown head and dark red bill and legs. In winter, no dark hood, but dark ear spot remains behind eye. Sexes alike. Young birds have more grey in plumage.

Food	on the Downs, almost anything – grass, worms, refuse.
Nest	not on the Downs. Generally on the coast in slight vegetation platform or scrape in the earth. Usually three eggs, laid each day from mid-April; incubation three weeks.
Locations	turf areas all over the Downs, particularly football pitches by the Sea Walls; and in Avon Gorge.

Black-headed gulls are small, neat and always moving: they rove the turf, often in company with herring gulls. They usually feed alongside starlings whom they attempt to dominate and control: I have seen a gull stride into a starling circle where two birds were fighting and then chase the most aggressive starling away from the area. Black-headed gulls themselves frequently squabble over food, chasing any of their number who has food and forcing them to drop it.

In the early morning, hundreds of these gulls fly along the Avon and on to the Downs. Sometimes they seem to change their mind, turn and pour back into the Gorge like milk boiling over.

These are noisy birds with a harsh, cackling call, hence their scientific name which means *laughing gull*.

Blue tit (*Cyanistes caeruleus*)

Status	resident.
Description	11.5cm. Blue upper parts, yellow below, black eye stripe, white cheeks. Black streak down lower body. Female slightly paler.
Food	caterpillars, insects, seeds, nectar, sap, pollen.
Nest	in holes in trees, filled with moss, dead leaves and wool and lined with hair and feathers. Lay from late April–May, clutch of 7–12 eggs. Eggs smooth white with purple spots. Incubation 13–16 days, fledged in about 20 days.
Location	Granny Downs; Dumps; Zoo Banks and shrub islands all around Downs.

Blue tits are charismatic little birds that announce their arrival loudly and make a great fuss of flying around. Young blue tits have yellow faces and stick together as a group, huddling up on branches, sometimes with other juvenile birds such as long-tailed tits and wrens.

Blue tits often nest in unusual places and I encountered a blue tit family nesting in a traffic sign on Westbury Road. The sign said *Bus Lane/Taxi 24 hours* and there was a light above it, all supported by a tube. I watched the parent birds disappear down the tube again and again, emerging to forage in the tree canopy and then popping back down the tube with caterpillars. An individual bird will roost in a tube such as this when it's cold because the light provides warmth.

Bullfinch (*Pyrrhula pyrrhula*)

Status	resident.
Description	male a plump bird (15cm) – pinkish red underparts, black cap and tail, white rump and grey upper parts, strong bill. Female same, but with pinkish-brown body.
Food	buds, fruit, seeds and insects.
Nest	flimsy nest of twigs, moss and lichen lined with roots. Lays late April–July, Four or five eggs pale green-blue with purple streaks. Incubation 14 days. Young birds fly after about 15 days.
Locations	wood edges, especially Ash wood; Fairyland; Zoo Banks; Circular Road woods.

Bullfinches are among my Downs' celebrity birds: the male is a gorgeous lipstick pink, yet he rarely displays himself for public view.

He cannot resist the sun, however, and can sometimes be glimpsed bathing in puddles, dissecting daisies with his mate on sunlit grass, or suddenly appearing on the outside of a shrub island. When he crosses from tree to tree, his mate will follow either several seconds later, or when the male is safely across. The pair stay together through the winter and some ornithologists believe that they mate for life.

The quiet, but distinctive call note *peu, peu* is as secretive as the bird itself.

Chaffinch (*Fringilla coelebs*)

Status	resident, joined by migrants.
Description	male, 14.5cm – grey crown and neck, brown back, with striking white double wing bars, pink underparts, green rump. Female – duller, all over olive/brown but similar wing patterns.
Food	mostly caterpillars in summer; seeds, shoots and berries in winter.
Nest	building (by female) begins in April/May – a neat nest of lichen, moss, grass and spiders' webs and lined with hair or feathers, in tree forks or shrubs throughout the Downs. Lays April–early June, 4 or 5 bluish eggs, sometimes splotched with purple. Incubation after 12 days. Young leave nest after two weeks.
Locations	Wooded fringes and hawthorn areas, especially Clifton Downs and Ladies Mile.

The chaffinch is a smart fellow, especially in the spring. He's not averse to admiration and stays in one place when singing so is easy to see through binoculars. The female is less stage struck. The chaffinch's contact call is *pink pink*, and his song is short and vibrant, ending with a twirl: I time the songs as an average of five a minute. Compare the Bristol Downs' song with chaffinch song elsewhere: chaffinch song has regional dialects usually evident in the length and panache of the twirl.

Chiffchaff (*Phylloscopus collybita*)

Status	Visitor from Africa March–September. Some over-winter here.
Description	Small warbler (11cm), olive brown above and cream below, dark stripe through eyes with pale stripe above, dark legs. Sexes alike. Easily identified by song – repeated *chiff chaff*.
Food	Insects.

Nest	Females build domed nest with side entrance in brambles, grass or dense vegetation. Lays late April–early May. Four to six white eggs with purple or brown speckles. Incubated for two weeks and young stay in nest for two weeks.
Locations	Dumps; Zoo Banks; Fairyland; Woods around Circular Road; Ash wood.

The Chiffchaff is a small bird with mighty message: *spring is here*. In 1780, the parson-naturalist, Gilbert White of Selborne, commented that the chiffchaff (not the cuckoo) was the true harbinger of spring.

Chiffchaffs sing from the treetops, favouring ash trees on the Downs, later moving down to the top of hawthorns. As they sing, they turn about like little weathercocks with bobbing tails. They frequently fly out to snap up an insect in flight, then return to the tree to feed on aphids and other insects: *phylloscopus* means *leaf explorer*.

Theirs is an earnest song, faithfully delivered, although I detect weariness in the notes during July.

Coal tit (*Periparus ater*)

Status	resident.
Description	small British tits, paler than relatives. 10.5/11.5cm. Grey upper parts with double white wing bar, buff/apricot underparts – with no central stripe. White stripe on back of head and white cheek patches. Slender bill.
Food	flies, beetles, moths, spiders, aphids, caterpillars, conifer seeds, beech mast.
Nest	in hole in tree or tree stump, sometimes taking over a disused rodent burrow. Neat cup of hair, feathers and moss. Lays April–early May, nine or ten eggs, incubation 14–16 days, fledge in 16–19 days. Independent in two weeks.
Locations	Fairyland; Circular Road woods; Promenade woods; Zoo Banks; Black Rock Gully.

Coal tits are neat little birds, similar to a great tit, though smaller, and brushed with watercolour rather than enamel.

Coal tits have the upside down acrobatic skills of the tit family, and they hover like hummingbirds to pick food from under leaves.

Troops of coal tits flutter restlessly from trunk to the top of the canopy, and suddenly decamp together to another tree. I've seen them on birch, oak, ash and yew.

They join mixed congregations of tits and small birds in winter, foraging for food: sometimes they stash food for winter, but forget where they have put it.

The song is a loud *zit tee* usually repeated four times, and is our best clue to their whereabouts.

Carrion Crow (*Corvus corone*)

Status	resident.
Description	47cm, glossy black plumage and large, rounded bill, square tail in flight. Sexes alike.
Food	carrion, eggs, chicks; invertebrates especially worms and beetles. Also eats fruit, seeds and discarded sandwiches.
Nest	in fork in tree, large cup of sticks held together with earth and moss. Lined with wool or hair. Lays April–May, four to six eggs, light blue with brown blotches. Incubation 19 days, fledge 32–36 days.
Locations	All around Downs, in wooded areas and on the grassland.

Carrion Crows are not as sociably inclined as rooks, and, apart from small flocks of juveniles, we usually encounter them singly or in pairs. On the Downs, they often sit on top of hawthorns, shifting from one leg to the other, reaching forwards as though about to vomit, and uttering *kraar* three or four times in quick succession. When they hear the crow, the small birds fall silent: crows are watchful and crafty thieves of eggs and chicks.

Crows (and rooks) shower in the early morning dew held by the long meadow grass.

Dunnock (*Prunella modularis*)

Status	resident.
Description	14.5cm. Grey head and breast parts, reddish brown flanks, streaked back and wings, thin bill. Sexes alike. Young birds spotted and look like juvenile robins.
Food	insects, worms, spiders, seeds in winter.
Nest	in hedge or bush in March. Cup of twigs, planet material, moss, lined with hair or feathers. Lays late March–early July, four or five light blue eggs. Incubated 14–15 days, fledged in twelve days.
Locations	near cover on Granny Downs; Fairyland; Dumps; Zoo Banks; scrub areas near Rangers Pound.

The Dunnock has his day in early spring, when for a short time he is the unrivalled singer with his sweet, cheerful lyrics, sung from a bush.

The dunnock is often described by reference to other creatures – for many years it was called the *hedge sparrow*, and his song is compared unfavourably with robins or wrens. Moreover, the ground-feeding creep and hop of the bird draws a comparison with mice. However, the complex social and sex life of this bird is now coming to light. This is far from ordinary and includes displacement of other birds' sperm during later mating, by rival males.

Goldcrest (*Regulus regulus*)

Status	resident, joined by migrants in winter.
Description	9cm. Upper parts olive green, under parts white buff. Adult male two pale wing bars and distinctive crown pattern, crest has deep orange centre. Thin bill. Female has yellow crest stripe.
Food	insects, spiders.
Nest	starts late April/May. Nest – tiny cup woven from cobwebs and lichen and suspended like hammock under branch of

conifer. Lays April–June. Seven to ten eggs, white or buff
with purple or brown speckles. Incubated for 14–17 days. In
nest for 16–21 days.
Locations   Conifers around the Downs; Zoo banks; Fairyland;
Observatory Hill.

Goldcrests are one of our two tiniest songbirds (the other is the
firecrest) and always on the move within a fairly limited area. They prefer
conifers and ivy-covered trees, and use their tiny bills to extract insects
from cracks in bark and between conifer needles. I hear their needle-thin
calls above me when I'm under yew canopies.

Their call is often confused with that of the treecreeper: both are high-
pitched and many folk cannot hear either.

Goldcrests can hover and they do this when taking food from a leaf or
twig. They frequently hang upside down to take food.

The firecrest (*Regulus ignicapillus*) is a rare relative of the goldcrest,
identified by its black and white eye stripes: in general, the plumage is also
brighter. Firecrests have been seen and photographed on the Zoo Banks.

Goldfinch (*Carduelis carduelis*)

Status   resident.
Description   adult bird has red face, white and
black head, brown body and
wide daffodil yellow wing
bars. White rump. Both sexes
alike. About 12cm. Young birds duller.
Food   seeds of weeds and birch, and insects.
Nest   built by female – woven cup of moss, grasses and lichens,
thistledown, plant material and spiders'webs. The nest is lined
with hair and feathers. Four to six blue-white eggs between late
April and early May. Chicks spend about two weeks in the nest
and stay with parents for seven to eight days after fledging.
Locations   Granny Downs; Durdham Down where they nest and roost;
Holm oaks near Water Tower; shrub islands around Downs.

Goldfinches are our loveliest finches with a pretty, bell-like, tinkling song, and a bouncy flight during which they continue their twittering conversations. They often feed on the ground and get yellow buttercup pollen on their heads. Goldfinches roost in the big holly tree on Durdham Down, and in the early morning, I've heard them chatting inside, while a blackbird kept watch.

Great spotted woodpecker (*Dendrocopos major*)

Status	resident.
Description	22cm–23cm. White and black, red under tail, white shoulder patches. Male has red patch on back of head, female lacks this. The bird has a very long, sticky tongue to extract food from crevices of bark. Bouncing flight: bird flaps three or four times, then folds wings back against body before flapping again. Call is an indignant *kick kick*.
Food	insects and larvae beneath bark, seeds, mainly conifer seeds.
Nest	mid-April, in hole in tree, usually at least 3m above ground. Lays May, between 4–6 smooth white eggs. Incubated in 15 days, and young fledged in three weeks.
Locations	Ash wood; Fairyland; Zoo Banks; Circular Road woods; woods below Observatory Hill; Trees of Wills Hall.

The great spotted woodpecker's short burst of territorial drumming is made up of around fifteen blows a second on a resonant surface such as a dead bough: the pitch varies according to the wood being drummed. It's a wonderful sound and sometimes, when the wind roars, the woodpecker drums, capturing and prolonging it like wind chimes. This activity, occurring between January and June, is also a way of keeping in contact with a mate, and we can usually hear an echoing drumming.

The great spotted woodpecker drums when trees are leafless so we have a chance of seeing it clinging to a bough or hopping up it using its stiff tail feathers for support. We need to be wily, however, because this bird doesn't like to be observed and will spiral around the tree evasively. I have often played this game with great spotted woodpeckers, especially in the Ash Wood.

Great tit (*Parus major*)

Status	resident.
Description	largest of tit family (14cm) glossy black head with white cheeks; yellow belly; central black stripe, blue-grey wings and tail. Females duller, with narrower stripe.
Food	mainly insects especially caterpillars in summer, buds, seeds, nuts, berries.
Nest	late March – cup of moss and grass, lined with hair in hole in tree or wall. Lays April–May, 7–9 eggs, hatch in 13–15 days and birds independent in a month.
Locations	Dumps; Zoo banks; Fairyland; Granny Downs; Circular Road woods.

The great tit is a smart, assertive bird with dozens of calls and phrases. If I hear a song unknown to me, it is usually that of a great tit. Its best known spring and summer call is *teacher teacher* (or *tea time, tea time* depending on your preoccupations).

The bird pecks at catkins and blossoms, and I recently saw an entire prunus (wild cherry) almost stripped of blossom. I hid and waited, expecting it to be a bullfinch that returned, only to see a great tit arrive and peck down the rest.

Outside the breeding season, great tits join forces with coal tits, blue tits, long-tailed tits and sometimes treecreepers in large feeding congregations around the Downs. The advantage of this large flock is that predators find it harder to focus on and attack individual birds.

Greenfinch (*Carduelis chloris*)

Status	resident, joined by winter migrants.
Description	Stout olive green finch (14.5cm) with lemon yellow wing-patches and tail edges. Female duller. Pink bill.
Food	seeds, sometimes insects.
Nest	Begins nesting late April/early May. Nest – twiggy cup, lined with moss, hair, feathers and plant stems. Lays early May–August. 4–6 pale green or grey-white with speckles. Hatch in 14 days and young spend 14 days in nest. Up to three broods. Often move locations for second and third brood.
Location	Shrub islands all round Downs.

The greenfinch's song announces its presence from late December – we hear a bell-like tinkering followed by a long wheeze. It's the pleasant background to spring and summer walks on the Downs and, as greenfinches often have two (sometimes three) broods, greenfinch families can be seen and heard on the Downs as late as September. It's a sociable bird, rarely venturing far from its group, and sometimes several birds nest in the same bush. Greenfinches and goldfinches often perch or fly together.

The greenfinch flies with an undulating flight, and when it stops to sing from a high perch, the yellow-green of its chest is made luminous by the sun.

Green woodpecker (*Picus viridis*)

Status	resident.
Description	Large woodpecker (30–33cm), olive green back, yellow rump, red crown. Male has red moustache, female a black one. Low, undulating flight. Has long tongue to extract ants and their eggs from nest.
Food	ants, grubs, and larvae of beetles, moths and flies.

Nest	hole in mature tree, nest at bottom of a long excavated chamber. Lays April–May, five to seven eggs, incubated for 18–19 days and young fed for three weeks.
Location	Granny Downs; Wills Hall area; Ash Wood; ash trees near Ladies Mile; Zoo Banks.

The green woodpecker is so exotic that it's sometimes mistaken for an escaped parrot. It's the town crier of the Downs' bird community, and the call itself is harsh and tonally similar to the neighing of a horse.

According to legend, the woodpecker calls when rain is due, but in practice, he calls just as it starts, and on sunny days just in case. The birds feed on ground, largely on ants, and look around frequently, beaks pointed skywards, to check the surroundings. I often see a green woodpecker banging away at frosty ground in the winter.

Green woodpeckers have two forward pointing toes and two backward, to help them climb trees. Their stiff tail feathers are used as a prop when climbing. These haughty-looking birds are easiest to spot when on the ground or in flight: in a tree they are masters of concealment.

Jackdaw (*Corvus monedula*)

Status	resident.
Description	fairly small (33cm) member of crow family with black wings, grey nape (headscarf) and blue eyes. Sexes alike.
Food	seeds, fruit, carrion, sometimes young birds and eggs.
Nest	in cliff holes and crevices on Downs' side of Bridge. Lays late April–May, three to seven eggs, light blue with grey and black flecks. Young hatch in about 18 days and fledge when one month old.
Locations	The Avon Gorge cliffs; lower ends of Clifton Down. Also watch from the Suspension Bridge and Peregrine Watch Point.

Jackdaws are fantastic flyers, wizards of the wind. They congregate along the Gorge sides, often perching on the fences.

When it's windy, jackdaws shoot high above the Gorge as though thrown by a giant hand, and then they dive like arrows, tumble and wheel in their darkly cloaked ballet, all the while clacking loudly. According to Konrad Lorenz (*King Solomon's Ring*) the master observer of jackdaws, the birds are good parents and never indulge in flying arrow stunts while guarding newly fledged young.

Jackdaws pair for life and sit together, preening each other and touching beaks. Their eyes are a piercing blue.

Jay (*Garrulus glandarius*)

Status	resident.
Description	pink/beige body (33cm), white rump, electric blue wing patch, streaked crest. Sexes alike.
Food	acorns, beechnuts, berries, molluscs, spiders, eggs and young of other birds.
Nest	towards end of March in nest fairly high in tree. Lays April–June, four or five green eggs; hatch in two weeks. Young spend around three weeks in nest, but stay with parents until autumn. Male and female often pair for life.
Locations	Westbury Park (Granny) Downs; amongst Horse Chestnuts around Durdham Down; Fairyland; Ash Wood; Observatory Hill; Zoo Banks.

The jay is our most exotic crow, and is often thought by excited non-birdwatchers to be a colourful and un-British rarity. It has a loud, high-handed treetop personality and a wary, silent self when nesting or on the ground hiding acorns. Should you hear an excruciating screech from the treetops, be assured that a jay is implicated, objecting to your presence or fighting a magpie, song thrush, or squirrel.

Jays cross from tree to tree singly like long-tailed tits, but with jerky wing beats: the white rump aids identification. The bright blue wing patch feathers are used in fly-fishing; I'm always looking for them in the grass. Young jays are a pretty, pearly pink.

Kestrel (*Falco tinnunculus*)

Status	resident.
Description	medium sized (34cm) bird of prey, chestnut back with grey head and long grey tail with black band. Female has chestnut stripes on tail with black band at end. Yellow legs. Female slightly larger.
Food	small mammals, birds.
Nest	April–May. Kestrels do not build a nest, but use tree cavities, ledges on buildings, scrapes on cliff ledges or old crows nests. Lays mid-April–May, four to six red-speckled eggs. Incubated for four weeks. Chicks fly at four to five weeks.
Location	Dumps, Zoo Banks, Fairyland, Ash Wood: Observatory Hill; Sea Walls area.

Kestrels are one of my celebrities of the Downs. A hovering kestrel is stunning: the bird's head remains still while the wings quiver with a ballet-like grace, and its wingtips float like silk in the wind.

When the bird repositions to hover over a different spot, it flaps its wings rapidly, then stops and is lifted a little way on the air. It looks as though it's settling in and getting comfortable. Kestrels face the head wind and match the air speed exactly.

In flight, the bird has the stiff appearance of a crossbow.

Long-tailed tit (*Aegithalos caudatus*)

Status	resident.
Description	tiny (14cm with long tail), black, white and pink. Sexes alike. In flight, resembles little ball with tail, or flying teaspoon. Allows proximity but always on the move so hard to photograph.
Food	insects, sometimes seeds and buds.
Nest	building starts in February, usually in thick brambles, shrubs such as hawthorn or gorse. Nest an oval dome of moss and

cobwebs, lined with around 2000 feathers. The nest can expand as the chicks grow. Lays late March–early May, 8–12 white eggs, hatching in about 16 days. Young birds leave nest after two to three weeks.

Locations   Wooded fringes, especially Westbury Park (Granny) Downs; the Zoo Banks; Fairyland; Observatory Hill.

The long-tailed tit is a joy. It's worth a trip at any time of the year to see them – they often fly in wind and rain, and are especially easy to see in leafless trees. The birds fly in family groups of sometimes more than 20 and cross from bush to bush in single file like Indian braves, gossiping away in *chirrs* and *trills*. Wonderfully agile, I've seen them swing upside down on catkins. Long-tailed tits are sociable, and failed breeders will help a relative with chick rearing.

Magpie *(Pica pica)*

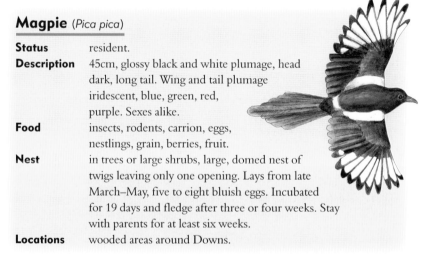

Status   resident.
Description   45cm, glossy black and white plumage, head dark, long tail. Wing and tail plumage iridescent, blue, green, red, purple. Sexes alike.
Food   insects, rodents, carrion, eggs, nestlings, grain, berries, fruit.
Nest   in trees or large shrubs, large, domed nest of twigs leaving only one opening. Lays from late March–May, five to eight bluish eggs. Incubated for 19 days and fledge after three or four weeks. Stay with parents for at least six weeks.
Locations   wooded areas around Downs.

Magpies used to arouse superstitious fear: now they make many people angry. Certainly, they can be aggressive birds – I've seen a magpie target a juvenile starling in a flock of youngsters and chase it until the starling dropped. I've also seen magpies raid the nests of small birds. But magpies are big, visible and noisy and carry out their activities largely without stealth, thus attracting the censure that other predators – such as cats and squirrels – escape.

Magpies fly as though aware of the responsibilities of their long tails and this leads to fascinating flying and landing techniques. In high winds, their tails are often blown over their heads.

In the spring, magpies gather in *parliaments* supposedly to resolve territorial conflicts: I've seen this occurring in Fairyland, and on the turf above Black Rock Gully.

Juvenile magpies are endearing as they run, hop and bounce along.

Mistle thrush (*Turdus viscivorus*)

Status	resident.
Description	larger than song thrush (27cm), grey/brown back, buff underparts, very heavily speckled with dark brown spots. White underwings distinguish from song thrush with yellow underwings. More upright stance than song thrush. Sexes alike.
Food	snails, slugs, worms, berries especially yew, holly and hawthorn, insects.
Nest	Lays February–June. Nest in fork of tree branch or bush, made of moss, grass, roots and mud, lined with dry grass. Four cream or light blue speckled eggs, incubated for 14 days, fledge after 14 days but young dependent on parents for two weeks.
Locations	All around Downs, but families move together on Durdham Down in July and August. Especially prominent in Christ Church Green.

The mistle thrush is another of my Downs' celebrities – for the astonishing carrying power of its song. One February morning when rain was lashing the trees and the wind was roaring, I could hear bird song coming from the middle of Clifton Down. It was a mistle thrush, shouting from the top of the giant ash.

Mistle thrushes are one of the first birds in the year to sing and are often known by the popular name *storm cock* because they sing through the storms of winter as well as fine days. Its song was thought to warn of a storm to come.

The song is a series of loud, ringing notes and there's a characteristic defiance to it.

The name of this thrush reflects its favourite food – mistletoe. Mistletoe sometimes occurs on the Downs on hawthorns and ash trees.

Nuthatch (*Sitta europaea*)

Status	resident.
Description	plump bird (14cm) resembling miniature woodpecker. Slate blue upper parts, apricot pink underparts. Strong, pointed bill and black stripe across eye. Short stubby tail. Sexes alike. The nuthatch can live for up to 11 years.
Food	mainly insects in summer, beech nuts, hazel nuts, acorns, seeds in winter.
Nest	holes in trees, customised – usually the entrance is made smaller by mud. Base of hole lined with dried leaves to cover the eggs. Lays April–May, six to nine white eggs, blotched with purple. Incubation period 16–17 days. Fledge after 23–25 days.
Locations	Fairyland; Promenade woods; Black Rock Gully woods, Granny Downs; Zoo Banks; Wills Hall area.

Nuthatches are snappy dressers touched by celebrity: they are the only European bird that walks down a tree trunk headfirst. They do this using their strong claws.

The bird's original name was *nut-hack* derived from its way of fixing nuts into the bark of a tree and hacking them open with its beak.

The grey and apricot colouring of this bird is exquisite in the sun – and I've noticed that when nuthatches fly between trees, they land on the sunny side of the trunk. One of my bird-watching high spots was seeing a parent nuthatch feeding two young on a low branch in Fairyland.

To encounter nuthatches, go over the Gorge to Leigh Woods where the Worshipful Company of nuthatches owns the woods!

Peregrine Falcon (Falco peregrinus) Male referred to as tiercel

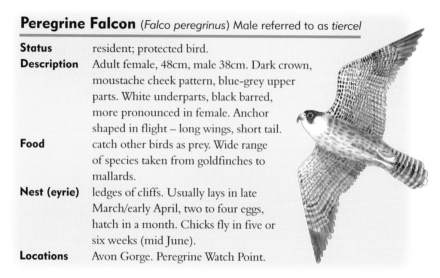

Status	resident; protected bird.
Description	Adult female, 48cm, male 38cm. Dark crown, moustache cheek pattern, blue-grey upper parts. White underparts, black barred, more pronounced in female. Anchor shaped in flight – long wings, short tail.
Food	catch other birds as prey. Wide range of species taken from goldfinches to mallards.
Nest (eyrie)	ledges of cliffs. Usually lays in late March/early April, two to four eggs, hatch in a month. Chicks fly in five or six weeks (mid June).
Locations	Avon Gorge. Peregrine Watch Point.

The peregrine falcons are the ton-up boys of the sky – our largest, most powerful falcons and arguably the most impressive hunting birds. They are also the fastest creatures on earth (up to 200mph – 320 kmph in a stoop). Peregrines usually kill in the sky, dropping onto their prey from a great height and breaking their neck or back with one blow of their talons. Prey is taken to a rock ledge or tree (*plucking tree*) to strip.

These falcons have a thrilling variety of flight behaviour: courtship flights, looping the loop, passing food to each other, and play fighting.

We have a good chance of seeing peregrines in aerial combat with many Downs' birds – I've seen them with swifts, gulls, rooks, buzzards, sparrowhawks, kestrels, jackdaws and ravens. In 1937, a peregrine killed a raven in the Gorge by stooping on it and breaking its neck. I've even seen them try to interest a heron in a spat, but the heron flew on serenely. Peregrines (like other birds of prey) are fierce defenders of territory. They fly out with grim determination to defend their territory from passing peregrines, and this time, the battle is real.

There is evidence (from the remains of their prey) that our peregrines also hunt the city by night, using the artificial lights to their advantage. Their prey includes migratory birds that only move around by night. Peregrines pair for life and can live for fifteen years.

Pied wagtail (*Motacilla alba*)

Status	resident.
Description	Rather horizontal birds. Adult (18cm) black and white plumage, black bib and cap, eyes on white patch; long tail, constantly wagging. Sexes similar. Flight like skimming stone.
Food	insects, molluscs, some seeds.
Nest	built by female, in holes in walls, log piles, banks, old nests of larger birds. Grassy cup, lined with hair and feathers. Lays April–June, five or six grey-white eggs, speckled with grey. Incubation 13 days, fledge 14 days.
Location	Around Sea Walls; near Water Tower; Durdham Down.

Pied wagtails cheer the bleakest day on the Downs. They arrive like exclamation marks with a surprised chirping, skim the turf like pebbles, land, wag and then shoot about like clockwork, stopping every now and then to wag some more. They are usually in pairs or threes, although in 2006, I counted 28 on the turf near the Seven Sisters on Durdham Down.

Pied wagtails are often (understandably) mistaken for miniature magpies. The birds appear to be attracted to bleak concrete areas, puddles and the edges of the pavement.

Raven (*Corvus corax*)

Status	resident.
Description	largest (64cm) member of crow family and largest species of perching bird in world. Larger than buzzard. Black with heavy, stout bill, wedge shaped tail in flight.

Food	carrion, small mammals, birds, insects, seeds and birds' eggs.
Nest	Large nest of twigs and sticks, thickly lined with moss and grass. One brood each year. Lays in February, usually 4–6 pale blue eggs, hatch in three weeks. Chicks can fly at about six weeks. Young stay with adults for 4–6 months after fledging.
Locations	Avon Gorge; Clifton Down towards Sea Walls.

Ravens with their rattling throaty *kronk kronk* bring the truly wild to the Downs: they are birds of lonely places. Once feared as a bringer of death and bad omen, ravens are now appreciated for their magnificence.

They are the first bird to nest, and they build on the Avon Gorge cliffs. Those of us watching from Peregrine Watch Point wait eagerly to see how many chicks hatch and whether they pass the stage where they are vulnerable to the jackdaws. And then comes the moment when the young birds must trust themselves to the air and what a comedy thriller this is! They shuffle to the edge of the nest, flap their wings, fall back and let the next chick try his courage.

Ravens are extraordinary flyers, turning on their backs or diving like arrows. The aerial battles between the peregrines and ravens are thrilling: both are masters of the air – and sometimes these battles occur over the Downs itself.

Ravens, like jackdaws, pair for life and once they have adopted a territory, they usually stay there.

Redwing (*Turdus iliacus*)

Status	winter visitor – October–April.
Description	smallest member of thrush family (21cm). Brown upper parts, white speckled breast with distinctive red patches under the wings and on the flanks. Characteristic creamy yellow eye stripe and pale stripe below cheek. Females and juveniles similar to adult male.
Food	berries – yew, hawthorn, holly. Also worms, snails and spiders.

| **Nest** | Not on the Downs: they breed in Northern Europe and a few pairs breed in northern Scotland. |
| **Locations** | The Granny Downs; Ladies Mile areas. |

Redwings are on my Downs' celebrity bird list for the beauty they bring to autumn and winter. They over winter here from Scandinavia, where they are one of the most numerous songbirds. Their high-pitched call, *tseeip* – can be heard as they migrate by night.

Redwings are small thrushes with yellow eyebrows and red patches under their wings. They are nervous birds with a ghostly presence and they fly as though being blown sideways.

Redwings feast on our hawthorn berries, and they transform the path through the Granny Downs into a ride of musical trees. When they congregate on the giant ash on Clifton Down, the tree looks as though it is in leaf again, and when these birds leave a tree, they do so singly, like flying leaves.

Few redwings breed in Britain, so we are unlikely to hear their song, but we do hear their sub song – a sweet, chatty warble. Walking through the Granny Downs one winter day, I heard what I thought to be the songs of dozens of these birds coming from brambles. I waited and eventually located a single singer: one redwing can conjure the music of an orchestra of birds.

Redwings are often seen in company with fieldfares, though there have been fewer of these of late on the Downs.

Robin (*Erithacus rubecula*)

Status	resident.
Description	Adult bird (14cm) red face and breast, with grey border. Upper parts and tail brown. Sexes alike. Both sexes sing.
Food	worms, spiders, seeds, insects, fruits
Nest	built by female, domed, made of grass and leaves. Lays March–June, four to six eggs, incubated for 12–15 days. Young birds leave nest after 14 days.
Locations	On wooded edges of Downs, and near houses.

Robins on the Bristol Downs appear predictable and friendly. A robin often stays near me until I leave his territory: he's curious, or seeing me off his patch.

Robins sing throughout the year, except for a short period in late summer when they moult. They sing at night, under the street lamps, and are mistaken for nightingales. They also sing a few notes after shooting stars explode into light and the mid-December meteor shower, the *Geminids*, is a good time to hear this.

Robins' sharp, spring song is regarded as different from their more melancholy autumn offering. Some experts dispute that this is the case, attributing it to our emotions rather than the quality of their song.

The chests of baby robins are speckled with gold: being duller than their parents helps them blend in and become less vulnerable to predators.

Rook (*Corvus frugilegus*)

Status	resident.
Description	45cm, purple-black, glossy plumage, thick, trouser-like thigh feathers, bare, light-grey face-patch, enormous grey bill, tail rounded when compared with that of carrion crow. Sexes alike.
Food	earthworms, insects, beetle larvae, seeds, nuts, small mammals, birds' eggs, nestlings and carrion.
Nest	begin March/April. Cup of sticks held together with soil and lined with leaves and roots, at top of tall tree and close to other rook nests. May renovate and reuse old nests. Lays late March–April, three to five blue green eggs with blackish speckles. Incubation, 16–18 days, fledge 30–36 days.
Locations	Ash Wood; Promenade woods; Clifton Down.

Rooks are sociable birds: they nest, feed and roost communally. I sympathise with folk who find rooks and crows indistinguishable, but the huge, grey beak of the adult rook and the white patch around the base of the bill are distinctive. Unfortunately, the first year juveniles don't have this – their faces and bills are dark, so they do look like carrion crows.

Although rooks would not seem an obvious candidate for beauty, their black gloss is shot with violet and sometimes dark red. Once, I watched a gentle faced, fluffy baby rook resting in the dappled shade of the Ash wood and thought I had never seen a bird more lovely.

Rooks walk carefully as though their baggy trousers are in danger of falling down.

Song thrush (*Turdus philomelos*)

Status	resident, joined by migrants in winter.
Description	adult 23cm, warm, earthy brown upper parts, buff, spotted belly with touch of golden brown. Prominent, robin-like eyes. Yellow plumage under wing. Sexes alike.
Food	insects, worms, berries, and snails – smashed open on 'anvil' stones or steps.
Nest	breeding begins in March; nest of thin twigs and grass usually in bushes, lined with mud. Lays March–June, three to five eggs, light blue speckled. Incubation around 14 days and young in nest for 13 to 17 days.
Locations	Ladies Mile; Ash Wood; Zoo Banks; Observatory Hill; Fairyland; Black Rock Gully; Dumps; Granny Downs. Thrush 'anvils' often found on paths in Fairyland.

The song thrush, although shy, is the most lyrical and varied songster: I still hear thrush phrases I have never heard before.

In December, song thrushes sing early in the morning from modest perches, to establish territories. As spring progresses, they sing from increasingly higher perches, and the treetops. Thrushes repeat each phrase between 3 and 11 times and the silvery descending phrases are the most heartrending of all.

Song thrushes fly low, and can be frustratingly hard to see, except on treetops in the sun.

Sparrowhawk (*Accipiter nisus*)

Status	resident.
Description	28–40cm. Female much larger than male; male smaller than a kestrel. Female brown upper parts, and grey brown barring on whitish underparts. Male grey/blue upper parts; barring on whitish underparts is orange/brown. Wings short, tail long with dark barring. Yellow eyes. Grey bill. Yellow legs and feet. Call is a shrieking *ke ke ke ke*. Sparrowhawks have a characteristic flip-flap-glide flight.
Food	female usually takes starlings, pigeons and thrushes, and male preys on smaller birds such as tits, finches, sparrows. Both sexes take small mammals and nestlings.
Nest	a flat platform of thin twigs in a tree. Lays May–June, 4–5 eggs (blue white with brown markings) incubated for 32–36 days. Chicks fledge after 24–30 days but are not independent until nearly a month later.
Locations	Granny Downs; Wills Hall area, Fairyland; Zoo Banks; Black Rock Gully; Peregrine Watch Point area and flying across the Gorge, sometimes engaging with the peregrines.

Sparrowhawks are stealthy, efficient birds of prey. Unlike kestrels, sparrowhawks do not hover, but watch from a hidden perch, then swoop like a ghost through the trees to take birds in flight. Other birds give a ripple of alarm calls as the sparrowhawk approaches and then fall silent as it passes by. Sparrowhawks rely on the advantage of surprise, but are capable of great bursts of speed and determination in pursuit, and of upside down manoeuvres to secure their quarry.

Prey is usually eaten on the ground or on a favourite perch and the sparrowhawk stands with both feet on its victim.

I'm haunted by an image of a sparrowhawk flying low over the meadow area near Peregrine Watch Point with the legs of a little bird hanging from the clutches of those enormous yellow feet.

Starling (*Sturnus vulgaris*)

Status	resident: large number of migrants from continental Europe arrive in the autumn to spend the winter here.
Description	21.5cm, in summer, male and female have yellow bills with pink at the base for females and blue for males. Their black plumage shines with purples and greens. In winter, they have white speckles above and below. Juvenile birds are a soft mousy brown. Both sexes sing throughout the year.
Food	insects, spiders, fruit, worms and snails. Probes for leatherjackets, and catches insects such as flying ants in the air.
	Nest often in woodpecker holes, but use any hole in tree, cliff or building. Lays April–May, four to seven light blue eggs. Hatch in 12–15 days. Fledge in 22 days.
Locations	Durham and Clifton Down. Often congregate near Water Tower.

The starling has a complex personality. His beauty is often overlooked but the bird has a becoming iridescence of green and purple; he mimics, clicks, squeaks and wolf whistles, but can also sings fine, poignant music. Singly, his flying is direct and unremarkable, yet the pre-roost swirls of the flock are awesome. Furthermore, the male, though regarded as a bully, is romantically reputed to bring flowers to the female on the nest: I spend much of my bird-watching life in spring hoping to see this.

In the late afternoon in the autumn, starlings gather to sing on the limes near the Downs Tea Rooms, or on the giant ash on Clifton Down: during the evening they will disperse to their roosts. On the Downs in winter, starlings rove the turf with gulls who tolerate them or not, according to how much food is available and how hard the ground is. In the summer, it's amusing to see starling parents loudly pursued by gangs of their young.

The starling may get its name from the little white stars that shine against its black feathers in the summer.

Swift (*Apus apus*)

Status	April–August visitor from Africa.
Description	16.5cm, sickle-shaped very dark, sooty brown wings, dark underparts. Strong, hawk-like toes. Tiny bill, wide gape. Sexes alike.
Food	airborne insects (up to 10,000 a day) spiders. Food gathered for young is kept in parents' throat pouches.
Nest	nest in roofs, in gaps in stonework, made of plant material picked from the air, leaves, winged seeds, feathers, stuck with together parents' saliva. Lays May–June, two or three smooth white eggs. Both parents brood, eggs hatch in about 19 days. Young fledge after 5–8 weeks: they never return to nest and seem to be ignored by their parents. Young swifts do not breed until they are four.
Location	The skies above the Downs.

Swifts belong to the sky. Usually, first swifts arrive around 27 April and suddenly squadrons are screaming through the sky.

When it's overcast, they swoop over the meadow grass looking for insects.

Swifts spend most of their life in the air and outside the breeding season, fly non-stop for nine months. They sleep, feed, and preen on the wing, and are the only bird to mate in the air.

At dusk, they circle up to between 1000 and 2000 metres where the air is warmer, and return to lower levels at sunrise. On a quiet night, we can hear their faraway screams.

Are peregrines or swifts the Grand Masters of the sky? Many times I've seen swifts in an Armada over the Gorge, the smaller birds twisting, turning and evading the falcons.

Swifts return to Africa in August.

A note about screaming. Screaming is actually a rapid succession of notes. It's believed that one reason for the screaming of swifts is to advertise their presence to other swifts that may join them: a large flock of swifts has an advantage in finding the best insect areas in the air. One of their folk names is *devil screamer*.

Tawny owl (*Strix aluco*)

Status	resident.
Description	large, pigeon sized (37–38cm) with round, dark face and huge, dark eyes. Chestnut brown above, pale streaked underside.
Food	field mice, voles, rats, shrews, birds, worms, large insects, frogs.
Nest	Shallow scrape in bottom of tree hole, hole in rocks, old crow's nest. Lays March to May, two to five white, rounded eggs. Incubation begins with first egg, so young vary in size. Young fly in about five weeks.
Locations	Fairyland; Ash Wood; Wills Hall area; Promenade woods.

Tawny owls have one of the most imitated bird calls – especially when haunted house sound effects are called for. Their *hoo-hoo-hoo … hoooo* is harsh and vibrating, as I can testify, having stood at the Gorge side, below an ash containing a tawny owl. The calls become even louder to compensate for the early morning traffic noise on the Portway.

In flight, tawny owls are silent and can pounce unheard by their prey, killing them with their huge talons, or biting them to death.

A flurry of alarm calls, and the sight of small birds bombarding part of a tree is often an indication that an owl is roosting there for the day. I've seen this on the Granny Downs and small birds seemed to come from far and wide to join in the mobbing.

Male and female pair for life.

Treecreeper (*Certhia familiaris*)

Status	resident.
Description	12.5cm, mottled brown above, white underparts, white eye stripe, long, thin downcurved bill. Long tail, divided into points at the end. Large claws. Sexes alike. Only species of treecreeper in Britain.
Food	beetles, earwigs, small moths, woodlice, spiders, seeds.

Nest	Behind ivy or loose bark on old trees, or in cracks in trunk. Nest is a loose cup of moss, dried grass on base of little twigs and lined with feathers, wool and bits of bark. Lays April–June, usually six eggs, white, speckled red. Incubated 14–15 days, fledged in 15 days.
Locations	Around horse chestnuts on Durdham Down; Fairyland; Circular Road Woods; Zoo Banks; Observatory Hill. Also often on sycamores.

Treecreepers are secretive birds and about the size of a goldfinch: I'm absurdly pleased when I've seen one. They look like feathed mice and spiral up and around a tree in a series of cartoon jerks, searching for insects. When they leave one tree, they fly to the bottom of a nearby tree and start the climbing up over again. On the Downs, I've seen them on silver birches, horse chestnuts, oaks, sycamores and ash trees.

The treecreeper's call is thin and high-pitched and not everyone is able to hear it. In the winter, the bird joins flocks of tits and small birds to forage for food.

When fledglings leave the nest, they are better at climbing than flying.

Willow warbler (*Phylloscopus trochilus*)

Status	visitor from southern Africa, April–September.
Description	12cm. Olive upper parts, yellow below, pale legs. Sexes alike. Moults twice a year.
Food	insects and spiders, fruit and berries.
Nest	On the ground amongst shrubs, in domed, feather lined nest of grass and moss. Lays late April–early May, six eggs, white with red speckles. Incubation 13 days, fledge after 13 days.
Locations	Dumps; Zoo Banks; Circular Road woods; Ladies Mile; Observatory Hill.

Willow warblers appear to be declining in numbers: none now nest on the Downs and that is a loss. However, they pass through the Downs in April and it is worth listening for their song: once heard, always in the heart. The willow warbler's song is like a verse in a summer poem. The song …

is beautifully strange
It is happy and yet so sad.[*]

A restless little bird, the willow warbler flutters at the ends of branches, and under leaves, searching for aphids.

Often confused with the chiffchaff (both are the colour of catkins) the easiest way to tell them apart is by their songs. One is mundane but reliable, the other a fragment of the sublime: both are an essential part of spring.

Baby willow warblers are yellow in the sunshine.

[*] P Taylor 1982

Woodpigeon (*Columba palumbus*)

Status	resident.
Description	largest (40cm) of Britain's pigeons, distinguished by white neck and wing patches. Grey body and bulging pink chest. White stripe across wings distinguish it from feral pigeons and stock doves. Sexes alike.
Food	mainly plant material on Downs – ivy berries, acorns, weed seeds, beech nuts, ash keys and buds. Also insects.
Nest	thin platform of twigs – often two white eggs can be seen from below. Observed breeding every month of year, but mainly July–September. Chicks in nest 29–35 days.
Locations	all around the Downs.

Woodpigeons have no tree craft, they crash around and often topple when reaching for berries, but they are stylish flyers: I love their soar and flap territorial and display flight, especially in the spring when they seem to be applauding. Juvenile pigeons have exquisite grey, pearly feathers and a gentle expression. The five-note (second stressed) call of woodpigeons, though monotonous, is the heartbeat of the Downs.

Wren (*Troglodytes troglodytes*)

Status	resident.
Description	9cm–10cm. Reddish brown plumage. Short, cocked tail. Sexes alike. Remarkably loud voice for its size.
Food	wide range of insects and other invertebrates.
Nest	From mid April, male builds several domed shape nests of moss, dried grass and leaves. Builds in ivy-covered tree trunks, crevices in walls and banks, tree and shrub islands. Female chooses one and lines it with feathers. Lays late April, five or six white eggs hatching after sixteen days. Young wrens fledge in 15–19 days.
Locations	Granny Downs; Zoo Banks; Fairyland; Observatory Hill; Promenade and all shrub islands and wooded areas around Downs.

The wren is referred to in European legend as *the king of birds* and there's bravura brilliance in the way this tiny bird sings from a hawthorn top, tail bobbing to emphasise his pronouncements. His song is loud and trilling and ends with a defiant flourish. The wren's aggressive notes are a loud churring and ticking.

Wrens are highly active, spending most of their time creeping through undergrowth in search of insects. On the Granny Downs, I watched a parent wren weaving through brambles like a bobbin, followed by four baby wrens scarcely larger than bumble bees.

Mammals

I'm convinced that, apart from squirrels, most animal life happens behind my back, so I often stop to look behind me. We need to be animal detectives and to know a few tracks and signs. Then we can see a path worn through grass overnight and be pretty sure we know which animal made it.

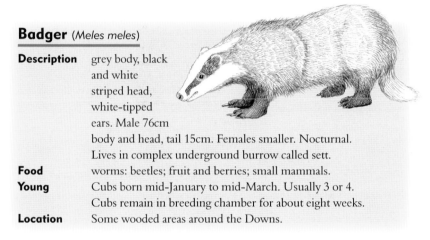

Badger (*Meles meles*)

Description	grey body, black and white striped head, white-tipped ears. Male 76cm body and head, tail 15cm. Females smaller. Nocturnal. Lives in complex underground burrow called sett.
Food	worms: beetles; fruit and berries; small mammals.
Young	Cubs born mid-January to mid-March. Usually 3 or 4. Cubs remain in breeding chamber for about eight weeks.
Location	Some wooded areas around the Downs.

Badgers on the Downs leave clues to their whereabouts, but are themselves hard to see. I've seen them before dawn, and heard amusing accounts from night security staff who have been astonished to see badgers ambling across the turf.

In the woods, there are little paths worn by badgers; also dung pits, snuffle holes and scratching trees. Many paths in woodland were originally made by these moonlight brocks, and then worn wider by humans.

After a rainy night, we can spot badger paths through the grass from and to the sett areas. I visited one of the setts regularly, leaving an apple beside it: the apples had disappeared by morning.

The word *badger* comes from the French *beucheur* meaning digger.

Bank vole (*Clethrionomys glareolus*)

Description	Smallest of UK voles, about 8.5cm head and body and tail 5cm. Blunt nose, rounded muzzle and small ears. Distinguishable from field voles by colour: bank voles are a reddy brown, field voles grey. Bank vole droppings are dark brown, field vole droppings are greenish. Active day and night. Nest in shallow burrows just below ground, lined with leaves, feathers, moss and grass. Sometimes nest under logs and tree stumps. Gregarious, large populations can occur in small areas.
Food	hazelnuts, fungi, berries, seeds, grass, moss and occasionally invertebrates such as worms and snails.
Young	Four or five litters, each with four or five babies between April and September. Young leave nest at 18 days old.
Location	Zoo Banks; Dumps; Fairyland.

Bank voles are one of the elusive little scuttlers that we hear (especially amongst dry leaves under bramble thickets) but seldom see. In my experience bank voles can be predictable. Having seen one emerge and then scuttle back, I wait and am sometimes rewarded by the re-emergence of a little head. Sometimes bank voles scuttle out onto the path when I am bird-watching in Fairyland.

The main predators of the bank vole are weasels, kestrels, foxes, sparrowhawks, tawny owls and cats. I often see kestrels hovering over areas I know to be populated by bank voles such as the Dumps.

BATS on the Downs by Mandy Leivers

Most people have an aversion to bats but once you get to know them you'll discover that they're wonderful, amazing creatures. Of the 4,500 species of mammal in the World, 1,200 are bats. That means almost a fifth of mammals are bats. 17 species of bat can be found in the UK*.

---

* Fact from the Bat Conservation Trust. For more information about bats and to find out how you can help bats visit www.bats.org.uk

Three kinds of bat that are frequently seen flitting around the Downs are common pipistrelles, noctules and serotines. Endangered lesser and greater horseshoe bats have also been seen roosting in caves, in the Avon Gorge.

The Promenade is one of the best places to see bats. You can simply go and watch them flitting about but its tricky to see them in the dark because they fly so quickly. If you take along a piece of equipment called a bat detector the experience is exhilarating. Bats find their prey by echolocating (basically they shout very loudly and listen to hear if the call comes back ie, has bounced off something like a tasty moth). Bats shouts are normally outside our range of hearing but a bat detector allows us to hear their calls.

Common pipistrelle
(Pipistrellus pipistrellus)

Description	medium to dark brown body. Body length 35–45mm, wingspan 190–250mm. Nocturnal.
Food	midges, mosquitoes, mayflies, lacewings and small moths.
Young	Mating takes place in the autumn (and occasionally in the spring). Females store live sperm in their bodies until the spring when the egg is fetilised. One pup born early June to mid-July. Pups are born naked and blind. Young are weaned at 6 weeks.
Longevity	Up to 16 years.
Location	Along the Promenade, around the Observatory and on the woodland edges along Circular Road.

Pipistrelles are the bats you're most likely to see flitting around trees and lampposts. They're the smallest bat in Britain. According to the Fauna Britannica, they're so small that, with their wings closed, they'd fit into a matchbox (please don't try this at home!). They have characteristic fast, jerky flight, with a charming habit of feeding just above head height. Once when we ran a bat walk on the Downs, two pips delighted the participants by circling just above their heads for about 5 minutes. I bet our warm bodies were attracting lots of insects that the bats were feeding on. It's been shown that a single pipistrelle can eat up to 3,000 insects in one evening.

There are actually three different species of pipistrelle; common, soprano and the rarer Nathusius' pipistrelle. At one time it was thought that common and soprano pipistrelle bats were the same species. However bat enthusiasts, listening to their calls on bat detectors, discovered that common pipistrelles call at a peak frequency of 45kHz and the sopranos' peak frequency is 55kHz.

Did you know that the name pipistrelle comes from the Italian word for bat 'pipistrello'?

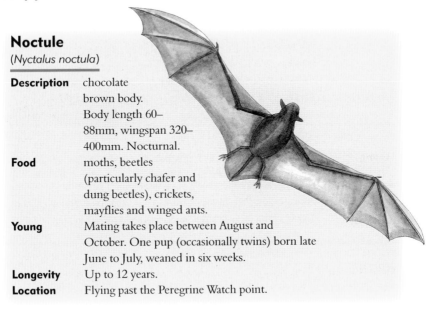

Noctule
(*Nyctalus noctula*)

Description	chocolate brown body. Body length 60–88mm, wingspan 320–400mm. Nocturnal.
Food	moths, beetles (particularly chafer and dung beetles), crickets, mayflies and winged ants.
Young	Mating takes place between August and October. One pup (occasionally twins) born late June to July, weaned in six weeks.
Longevity	Up to 12 years.
Location	Flying past the Peregrine Watch point.

Noctules are one of the first bats to appear in the evening, sometimes before sunset. They feed at two points during the night; for about two hours at dusk and for around half and hour at dawn. It's been shown that they fly over 6 miles (10 km) to find food. Compared to pipistrelles they are big bats. They have long, narrow wings and tend to fly high above the tree-line with direct powerful flight, making speedy turns and diving down to grab insects. They've been clocked reaching speeds of 30mph (50km/h).

Noctules echolocate between 20–45Hz with a peak at 25kHz and on a bat detector their call sounds like 'chip chop – chip chop'.

In late summer, male noctules behave a bit like spring birds or red deer. They set up and defend a territory from other males and attract a 'harem' of 4–5 (but sometimes up to 20) female bats making loud, shrill calls. They also produce a strong smell to draw in the ladies!

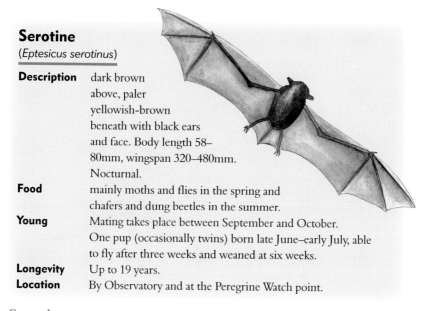

Serotine
(*Eptesicus serotinus*)

Description	dark brown above, paler yellowish-brown beneath with black ears and face. Body length 58–80mm, wingspan 320–480mm. Nocturnal.
Food	mainly moths and flies in the spring and chafers and dung beetles in the summer.
Young	Mating takes place between September and October. One pup (occasionally twins) born late June–early July, able to fly after three weeks and weaned at six weeks.
Longevity	Up to 19 years.
Location	By Observatory and at the Peregrine Watch point.

Serotines, like noctules, appear early in the evening, often emerging when it is still relatively light. They have broad wings, are highly manoeuvrable often flies in loops in open areas.

On a bat detector their call is syncopated (sounds a bit like a jazz drummer). These bats echolocate between 15–65kHz with a peak at 25–30kHz. Children and some adults can hear these bats calling without a bat detector.

They chew large beetles on the wing, allowing wing cases to drop to the ground or go to a perch to devour them.

Eptesicus means 'house-flyer' as it's often seen flying near and roosting in houses

Brown rat (*Rattus norvegicus*)

Description	Head and body average 18cm. Coarse brown or greyish brown fur, pale undersides. Long scaly tail almost as long as head and body combined. Largely nocturnal. Home range 50 metres diameter. Live in burrows often under tree roots.
Food	omnivorous –anything.
Young	Breeding throughout year, 5 litters a year – average of 8 young, weaned after a month. In good conditions they can have 13 litters a year.
Location	Fairly widespread.

The brown rat is a creature of habit and is easy to track by following one of its well-worn paths (*rat runs*) through the grass into the undergrowth. A few of them have taken to climbing a little way up shrubs to snuffle berries and this is visible in the winter.

Brown rats have only been in this country for 300 years, having arrived here on board ships from the Far East: they are highly adaptable creatures.

The wise, beloved Ratty of Kenneth Grahame's *The Wind in the Willows* was not a rat, but a water vole.

Field vole (*Microtus agrestis*)

Description	Head and body length 10cm. Tail 4cm. Grey-brown fur, pale underparts, small eyes and ears, blunt nose and short tail. Active day and night, although largely nocturnal in summer. Live in underground tunnels.
Food	stems and leaves of grasses. Also nibble tree bark but this may be to mark territories.
Young	Between March and September. Nest of dry grass, hidden in grass tussock or under logs. 4–6 young, weaned at 16 days. Up to 7 litters a year.
Location	Zoo Banks; Dumps; Meadow areas near woods.

Field voles are amongst the most numerous of British mammals and are regarded as vitally important because so many predators depend on them for food. On the Downs, these predators are foxes, weasels, tawny owls and kestrels.

Field voles scuttle along a connecting network of runways in the grass to reach their tunnel entrances. They leave an unpleasant scent (made by urine and small piles of poo) along these runways to warn off other voles. The urine emits ultraviolet radiation easily seen by birds of prey.

Male field voles hold a small territory and defend this against other voles with a good deal of angry chattering and squeaking.

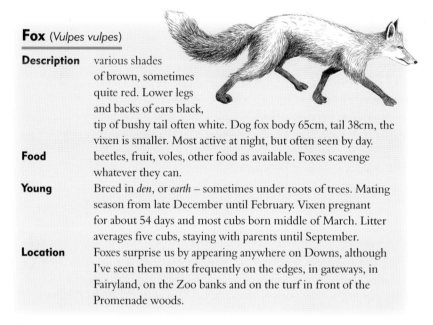

Fox (*Vulpes vulpes*)

Description	various shades of brown, sometimes quite red. Lower legs and backs of ears black, tip of bushy tail often white. Dog fox body 65cm, tail 38cm, the vixen is smaller. Most active at night, but often seen by day.
Food	beetles, fruit, voles, other food as available. Foxes scavenge whatever they can.
Young	Breed in *den*, or *earth* – sometimes under roots of trees. Mating season from late December until February. Vixen pregnant for about 54 days and most cubs born middle of March. Litter averages five cubs, staying with parents until September.
Location	Foxes surprise us by appearing anywhere on Downs, although I've seen them most frequently on the edges, in gateways, in Fairyland, on the Zoo banks and on the turf in front of the Promenade woods.

Foxes arouse mixed emotions, although us Bristol folk often have a soft spot for the foxes that sunbathe on our garages and roofs, and stroll along our roads, bold as brass, when we are leaving for work.

One sunny morning, I saw a fox and two cubs playing on Clifton Green and then later, the same family sparring with two magpies. Foxes on the Downs are fairly predictable, and at dawn, several of them sit in the middle of the gateways of the large Rockleaze houses.

Foxes moult during the summer and look rather tatty. During October to January, they are fine fellows with full, glossy coats.

It's always worth giving a ginger coloured dog a second look on the Downs – I've been surprised to see a dog without owner or collar – until I realise it's a fox!

Grey squirrel (Sciurus carolinensis)

Description	bushy tail, white underparts and untufted ears. About 25cm head and body, tail 20cm. Silvery grey in winter, reddish brown in summer. Diurnal – most active at dawn and dusk. Lives in treetop summer nest (*drey*) for breeding, and more robust winter drey close to trunk of tree.
Food	fungi, acorns, beech mast, nuts, leaves, shoots, flowers and buds. Sometimes surplus food is buried ready for winter. This is often not recovered and aids seed dispersal. Squirrels will also eat birds' eggs and young.
Young	born in twiggy treetop drey in spring or early summer. On average three young who disperse at about eleven weeks.
Locations	Trees at edges of the Downs.

Grey Squirrels are the most frequently seen wild animal on the Downs: they bound, climb and leap as though made of furry air. The name *squirrel* means *tail that casts a shadow*: Squirrels use their tails as a sunshade, to communicate with other squirrels, to flick when they are annoyed, and as a blanket in the cold.

Squirrels sit on posts and walls: I've seen five sitting together on the wall outside Wills Hall. They also like to feed sitting on logs and tree stumps (*squirrel tables*) that become covered in nutty debris: there are several of these in Fairyland.

Often a kerfuffle in a treetop means that a squirrel is attacking a nest for eggs or nestlings. Squirrels themselves have many calls, some involving a loud chirring.

Young squirrels practise hopping between branches and between trees: they often fall but can land safely from heights of about 7m.

The summer coat of the grey squirrel is brown. The sun illuminates this to red, and passers-by often tell me they have just seen a red squirrel on the Downs. This is unlikely as the nearest red squirrels are on Brownsea Island.

Hedgehog (*Erinaceus europaeus*)

Description	Spiny coat (adult has about 5000 spines). Rough hair on face and underparts. About 25cm long. Rolls into a ball to deter predators. Hibernates in winter.
Food	worms, beetles, caterpillars, birds' eggs, snails, slugs.
Young	Average of four young born between April and September in nest of grass and leaves. Young are born blind and pink with a coat of soft white spines which are under the skin to protect the mother giving birth! The spines emerge within hours. A second coat of dark spines emerges after about 36 hours and later, a third set develops. By six weeks old they have more than 2000 spines. By 11 days the young can curl into a ball, and their eyes open after 14 days.
Location	Fairyland; Granny Downs; Zoo Banks; Wills Hall area.

Hedgehogs are Britain's only spiny mammal and are much featured in folk tale and children's stories. They are mainly active by night and I've seen a mother with two young at dawn on Durdham Down, moving surprisingly quickly towards the holly tree where they were nesting.

I've also seen one ambling along Ladies Mile, fortunately keeping to the pavement: I walked in slow motion, a couple of steps behind, until the hedgehog turned left into the bushes.

Roe deer (*Capreolus capreolus*)

Description	Species native to Scotland, introduced into rest of UK in 19th Century, after it became extinct in 18th Century. Summer coat sleek and red. Winter coat grey/brown or black. Short tail, white rump patch. Buck has antlers, shed in November or December. New growing antlers are protected by woolly skin (*velvet*) and buck looks as though has socks on head. Most active at dawn or dusk.
Food	tree shoots, brambles, grass.
Young	Mating takes place in July and August. Young (*kids*) born the following May or June. Twins common. Kids have white spots which disappear after six weeks. Location: Leigh Woods and the Avon Gorge. Can sometimes be seen from the Downs.

Roe deer are graceful and appealing, but they are also elusive. Sightings of roe deer on the Downs itself are increasing but unpredictable. There is, however, a more reliable chance of seeing them through binoculars in the quarries opposite Peregrine Watch Point. In late summer, the parent deer sometimes leave their kids half concealed in these quarries for safety, visiting them at intervals through the day.

Binoculars will help us see deer hoof prints in the Avon mud, and if we are lucky, deer coming to drink from the river or strolling along the cycle path. On numerous occasions, deer have been spotted swimming across the river, in high tide.

Shrew (Common shrew) (*Sorex araneus*)

Description	about 7.5cm with long, pointed nose and small round ears. Tail about 4cm. Long whiskers. Red-tipped teeth. Winter fur dark brown, summer fur light brown. One of most common British mammals. Active day and night. Spends most of life underground.

Food	worms and insects, woodlice and slugs.
Young	Several litters of six or seven young a year, from April onwards. Young independent at one month old.
Location	Fairyland; Zoo Banks; Ash Wood; Circular Road Meadows and Woods.

Shrews are easy to identify because of their long noses. I encountered one as I walked home through the Granny Downs on a moonlit winter night. The shrew was moving quickly around the base of an ash. It was foraging restlessly as this little creature will starve to death if it goes without food for more than three hours.

The shrew nests below ground in thick vegetation and is solitary: shrews are aggressive to each other and squeak piercingly in their territory battles. Shrews can actually produce ultrasound, which may be used as a primitive form of echolocation.

Interestingly, shrews are closely related to moles and hedgehogs. The Latin name *araneus* means spider and this refers to an old belief that shrews were poisonous, like spiders.

Weasel (Mustela nivalis)

Description	smallest British carnivore. Size variable – 20cm head and body, tail 2–8cm. Males larger than females. Ginger brown fur, white underparts. Thin body, short legs. Looks like long ginger mouse. Largely nocturnal.
Food	mice, voles, birds' eggs, especially tits' eggs, and nestlings.
Young	born in spring, stay with parent for two months to learn hunting skills.
Location	Anywhere near shrub cover and I have seen them most frequently in Fairyland and near the Dumps. Sometimes seen in hedges by Peregrine Watch Point.

Weasels are ferocious hunters and are part of the Downs' wildlife that happens when I'm not looking. I see them when I've turned to look behind me – and there's a slender weasel bounding between shrub islands. We're unlikely to see many because individual weasels have a territory of between ten and twenty acres.

Unlike the *band of weasels, armed to the teeth … of The Wind in the Willows*, weasels are largely solitary and live in the dens of former prey: their long thin shape enables them to go into underground tunnels for food.

This sleek little hunter is itself hunted, by owls, kestrels and foxes.

Wood mouse or long-tailed field mouse (*Apodemus sylvaticus*)

Description	orange-brown fur on back, pale grey fur underneath. 8–11cm. Large, bulging eyes, big ears, long hairless tail. Large hind feet. Mostly nocturnal. Dig and live in underground burrows. Go into torpid state in winter. Acute sense of sight and smell.
Food	nuts, fruits, seeds, fungi, snails, worms and insects.
Young	breeding season – March to November. Up to four litters, each of average of 5 young, independent after three weeks.
Locations	Zoo Banks; Fairyland; near Peregrine Watch Point.

Wood mice are one of the most widespread and abundant of British mammals, yet the least seen: they leave their burrows under cover of darkness. On the Downs, they are vulnerable to weasels, kestrels, foxes, badgers and cats – and a major food source for the tawny owl. Wood mice are highly active and able to leap like kangaroos to escape predators, using their long back feet. They can also shed their tail if it is gripped anywhere other than the base, allowing the mouse to escape. The skin does not grow back – instead the area of the tail dies and falls off.

In the winter, they often share their nest with several others to keep warm, and their complicated burrow system is used by consecutive generations, like badgers.

The Bristol Downs:
a natural history year

I have so many beautiful wildlife encounters on the Bristol Downs that my life feels enchanted. On my journeys I meet others who smile and say, *isn't it lovely up here; aren't we lucky to have all this*. It's a privilege to write about a landscape so widely beloved.

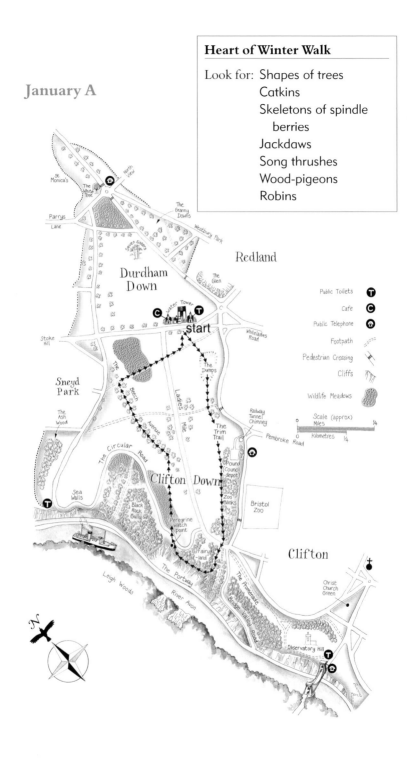

January A

Heart of Winter Walk

Look for: Shapes of trees
Catkins
Skeletons of spindle
berries
Jackdaws
Song thrushes
Wood-pigeons
Robins

St. Monica's
The White Tree
North View
Parrys Lane
The Granny Downs
Westbury Park
Redland

Seven Sisters
Durdham Down
The Glen

Stoke Hill
Water Tower
start
Whiteladies Road

Sneyd Park
The Beech
Ladies Mile
The Dumps

The Ash Wood
Avenue
Railway Tunnel Chimney
The Trim Trail
Pembroke Road

The Circular Road
Clifton Down
Pound (Council depot)

Sea Walls
Black Rock Gully
Zoo Banks
Bristol Zoo

Peregrine Watch Point
Fairy-land
Clifton

Leigh Woods
The Portway
River Avon
The Promenade
Bridge Valley Road
Christ Church Green

Observatory Hill

Public Toilets **T**
Cafe **C**
Public Telephone

Footpath
Pedestrian Crossing
Cliffs

Wildlife Meadows

Scale (approx)
Miles 0 — ¼
Kilometres 0 — ¼

N

What to Look for in **January**

As the day lengthens
So the cold strengthens

Small birds fly together, hunting for food and hoping to confound sparrowhawks with the difficulty of targeting a single bird among so many. One January, on the Granny Downs, I stood under a large, noisy gathering. Well over a hundred blue tits, great tits and long-tailed tits were flying from hawthorns to limes. Other passers-by were staring up, as astonished as I was.

January and in my heart, spring begins. There's encouragement for this in the sweet violets, the green buds of sycamores and in the bright songs of robins. But frost grips and the sunlight is as brittle as the ice on the puddles. This is the depth of winter: prepare for wonderland.

A frozen landscape, spellbound by frost. White, feathery turf crunches underfoot. Mist hides the treetops of Ladies Mile. The volcano sun rises behind the silhouetted tree branches on the Zoo Banks. Great tits, chaffinches and blue tits race around, calling. Woodpigeons shift about on branches. The sunlit turf sparkles like diamonds. Mist floats on the river, and gulls drift like snowflakes.

Sometimes snow takes us to a newfound land. Usually, though, it's a fleeting glimpse of white, and the fast-melting remnants of snowmen.

Birds surprise us. Male and female raven soar, dive and roll above the turf near the Sea Walls: they partner the wind with grace, and call like throaty ducks. Ravens are the first birds to pair and have often settled on their nest in the cliffs by the end of the month.

Song thrushes sing with increasing urgency: I've studied birds all my life, and yet still hear thrush phrases new to me.

The trees along Ladies Mile are musical with the calls of redwings, winter visitors from Northern Europe. These are elusive birds, half way in size between a robin and a thrush, with pink patches under their wings, and with pale eyebrows: they are especially partial to our hawthorn berries. Dozens of them sit in the ashes or limes and these trees look as though they are in leaf again.

Sun spotlights green woodpeckers banging the ground for ants, and then lifting their heads, beaks high, to look around. Green woodpeckers are vigilant and curious, and have fixed ideas about how much human proximity to allow: when we overstep the mark, they'll be off with a flight that dips as though their wings are straining to carry their bodies. In January, they utter a few notes of their laughing call. This becomes harsher as the year progresses.

A kestrel balances on the top twig of the ash by the Dumps, hump-backed, staring down. Robins and great tits sing. Pied wagtails turn up in bleak places. Starlings lurk around the Dumps and imitate the wheeze of greenfinches. Crows vie for perches on the water tower.

Tree buds remain tightly closed. Hazel catkins are tight and etched with red. On the branches of male yews, rows of little yellow dots appear – these are the pollen-bearing flowers. Woodpigeons devour ivy berries as they ripen.

Flowers begin and the path around Fairyland is way-marked by the tiny leaves of barren strawberry. Alexander and cow parsley leaves grow around shrubs. Celandine leaves (plain or spotted) appear in Fairyland, near Wills Hall and around the bases of lime trees in the Granny Downs. There's a thick and fragrant patch of purple sweet violets around an elder near Ladies Mile: the leaves smell as well as the flowers.

Jelly ear fungus, brown and rubbery, occurs on elder branches.

A red admiral butterfly flies over the Granny Downs rooftops, pointed out by one passer-by to another.

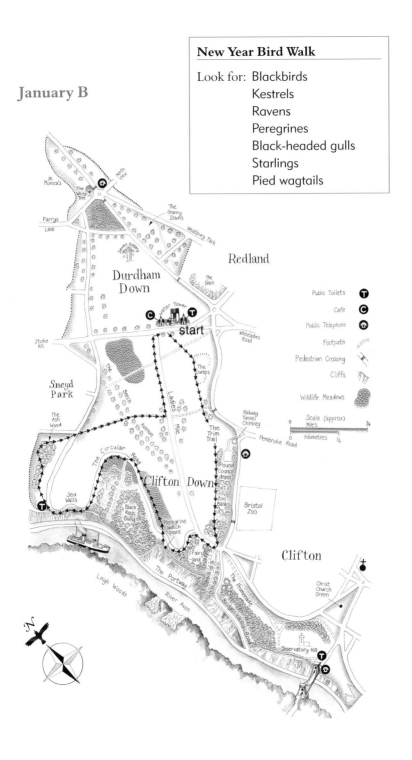

New Year Bird Walk

Look for: Blackbirds
Kestrels
Ravens
Peregrines
Black-headed gulls
Starlings
Pied wagtails

January B

St Monica's
North View
The White Tree
Parrys Lane
The Granny Downs
Westbury Park
Seven Sisters
Redland
The Glen
Durdham Down
Water Tower
start
Whiteladies Road
Stoke Hill
The Dumps
The Beech
Sneyd Park
Ladies Mile
Railway Tunnel Chimney
The Ash Wood
Avenue
The Trim Trail
Pembroke Road
The Circular Road
Pound Council depot
Clifton Down
Sea Walls
Black Rock Gully
Zoo Banks
Bristol Zoo
Peregrine watch point
Fairy-land
Clifton
The Portway
Leigh Woods
River Avon
Bridge Valley Road
The Promenade
Christ Church Green
Observatory Hill

Public Toilets
Cafe
Public Telephone
Footpath
Pedestrian Crossing
Cliffs
Wildlife Meadows
Scale (approx)
Miles
Kilometres
N

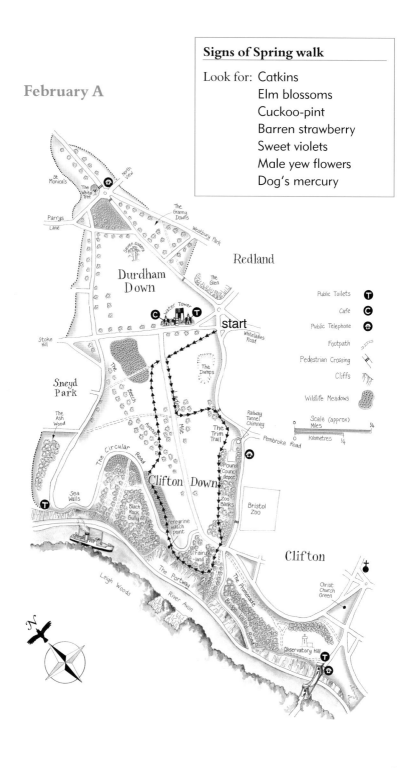

February A

Signs of Spring walk

Look for: Catkins
Elm blossoms
Cuckoo-pint
Barren strawberry
Sweet violets
Male yew flowers
Dog's mercury

Redland

Durdham
Down

start

Stoke
Hill

Sneyd
Park

The Ash
Wood

Clifton Down

Sea
Walls

Black
Rock
Gully

Peregrine
watch
point

Fairy-
land

Bristol
Zoo

Clifton

Christ
Church
Green

Leigh Woods

River Avon

The Portway

Observatory Hill

St
Monica's

The
White
Tree

North
View

Parrys
Lane

The
Granny
Downs

Westbury Park

Seven Sisters

The
Glen

Water Tower

Whiteladies
Road

The
Dumps

Beech

Avenue

Ladies Mile

The
Trim
Trail

Railway
Tunnel
Chimney

Pembroke Road

Pound
Council
depot

Zoo
Banks

The Circular Road

Bridge Valley Road

The Promenade

Public Toilets

Cafe

Public Telephone

Footpath

Pedestrian Crossing

Cliffs

Wildlife Meadows

Scale (approx)
Miles
Kilometres
¼
¼

N

What to Look for in **February**

February fill the dyke
Either with the black or white

A circle of rooks, and one in the middle parading around
with a paper cup in his beak. Now he puts the cup on the
ground and pecks at the remains of food in the bottom.
Ah – a challenge! One of the other rooks pounces on
him and grabs the cup. And now *he* parades around with
it before pecking at the food in the bottom...

February brings more gales and frost, and a white sun peeps
through the bleakness. But there's something in the air; sweet misty
mornings, warm birdy afternoons; swinging, pollen-filled catkins, and the
audacious flying of the jackdaws.

Birds are wind-blown; gulls sit like wedges on the turf, facing the
wind. Peregrines climb the gale, spiralling out of sight. Jackdaws fling
themselves into the Gorge and twist and fall: sometimes they circle
together like a Ferris wheel.

Magpies find it difficult to control their tails, yet persist in seeking out
high perches. Robins stay low, scampering under shrubs like restless
leaves. On the Zoo Banks, a great spotted woodpecker calls by drumming
on wood, bursts of percussion accompanying the wind. Later, there's more
drumming, in the Ash Wood across the Downs: this time the call begins as
the wind subsides, prolonging the music.

In calmer moments, dunnocks sing sweetly from the top of hawthorns.

Ravens are already on the nest, a twiggy contrivance on the side of a
quarry. Mistle thrushes, too, will be on the nest by the end of the month.

Elsewhere, friskiness begins: wrens explode from bushes and chase each
other – twice they have mistaken me for a tree and hurtled round my

ankles. Great tits dash through branches and twigs, calling noisily: blue tits follow, twittering with excitement. Green woodpeckers lurch after each other. Goldfinches parade their enamelled colours. On high perches, greenfinches are uttering their *tinkle and wheeze*. Blackbirds are self-important and clucky. Chaffinches practise their opening phrases – they will perfect the final flourish in a few weeks.

Jays, usually secretive, survey the scene from open perches. Bullfinches, even more furtive than jays, show themselves in the sun. Magpies patrol. Nuthatches announce themselves in Fairyland.

In the comings and goings, fluffy feathers are shed, and long-tailed tits dash from bushes to catch them, or pick them from the brambles. These pretty pink and black birds construct a nest of feathers, spiderwebs, moss and lichen: the nest expands as the chicks grow. Later in spring, female wrens will look for feathers to line the domed nest that they choose from the selection the male wrens present to them.

Flowers delight us. Celandines open in the sunshine. Barren strawberry flowers in Fairyland, and looks like golden-hearted dewdrops. The sweet violet bower near Ladies Mile has several hundred purple blooms. In Fairyland, dog's mercury emerges bent, like safety pins and its emerald green flowers light the woodland floor. Glossy cuckoo-pint leaves (plain and purple-spotted) unfurl beneath bushes. Red-rimmed daisies are scattered across the turf. Primroses flower on the Zoo Banks.

The leafless elms have a red aura created by their mass of flowers. English oak buds have swollen and the buds of horse chestnuts are amber and shiny.

Female hazel flowers are fiery red stars and catkins (the male flowers) frisk in the breeze, releasing pollen. Male yews are covered with fragrant mimosa-like flowers: these also send clouds of pollen into the air, and on to the surrounding yew needles, silvering them.

Squirrels are courting, pelting after each other up and down trees. At night, mating foxes scream across the Downs: in the daytime, individuals sunbathe below the cliffs. Badgers have cubs in their setts.

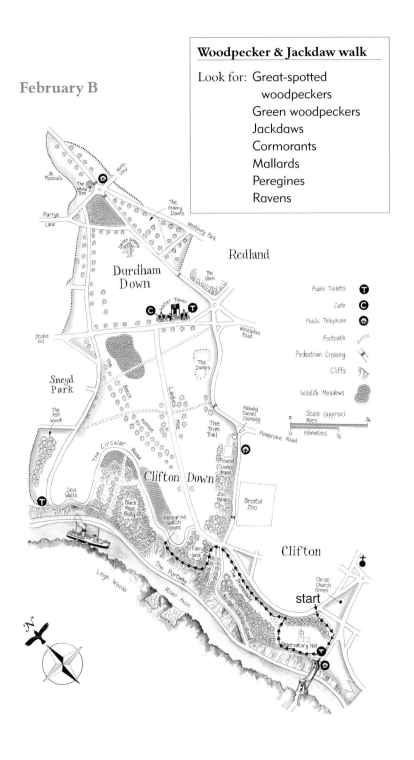

February B

Woodpecker & Jackdaw walk

Look for: Great-spotted
            woodpeckers
          Green woodpeckers
          Jackdaws
          Cormorants
          Mallards
          Peregines
          Ravens

St.
Monica's

North
View

The
White
Tree

Parrys
Lane

The
Granny
Downs

Westbury Park

Seven sisters

Redland

Durdham
Down

The
Glen

Water Tower

Stoke
Hill

Sneyd
Park

The
Beech

The
Ash
Wood

The
Dumps

Whiteladies
Road

Ladies
Mile

Avenue

The Circular Road

Railway
Tunnel
Chimney

The
Trim
Trail

Pembroke Road

Sea
Walls

Clifton Down

Black
Rock
Gully

Peregrine
watch
point

Pound
(Council
depot)

Zoo
Banks

Bristol
Zoo

Public Toilets

Cafe

Public Telephone

Footpath

Pedestrian Crossing

Cliffs

Wildlife Meadows

Scale (approx)
Miles
¼

Kilometres
¼

Clifton

Christ
Church
Green

start

Fairy-
land

The Portway

Leigh Woods

River Avon

The Promenade

Bridge Valley Road

Observatory Hill

N

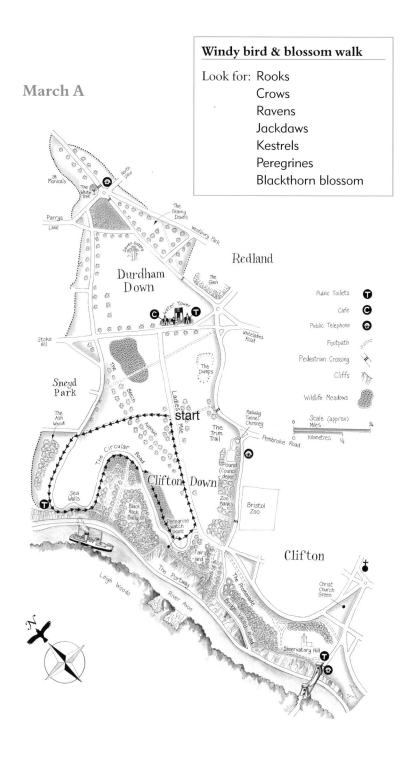

March A

Windy bird & blossom walk

Look for: Rooks
Crows
Ravens
Jackdaws
Kestrels
Peregrines
Blackthorn blossom

Redland

St Monica's
North View
The White Tree
The Granny Downs
Parrys Lane
Westbury Park
Seven Oaks
Durdham Down
The Glen
Water Tower
Stoke Hill
Whiteladies Road
The Beech
The Dumps
Sneyd Park
The Ash Wood
Ladies Mile
start
Railway Tunnel Chimney
The Trim Trail
Pembroke Road
The Circular Road
Avenue
Clifton Down
Pound (Council depot)
Sea Walls
Black Rock Gully
Zoo Banks
Bristol Zoo
Peregrine watch point
Fairyland
Clifton
Christ Church Green
Leigh Woods
The Portway
River Avon
The Promenade
Bridge Valley Road
Observatory Hill

Public Toilets
Cafe
Public Telephone
Footpath
Pedestrian Crossing
Cliffs
Wildlife Meadows

Scale (approx)
Miles
Kilometres
¼
¼

N

What to Look for in **March**

In the beginning or in the end
March its gifts will send

Here comes a buzzard from Leigh Woods, intent on living dangerously. It lands in the jackdaws' tree. Outraged jackdaws force the buzzard to take off again and now both peregrines scramble to defend their airspace. But a second buzzard joins the first, and now the ravens take them on. Both buzzards retreat to Leigh Woods, escorted by ravens.

M arch holds hands with winter and spring. Icy winds blow, but sunshine is stronger and the land warms: violets flower and birds sing. Folk tell me *it's going to happen, spring really is coming*. There's relief in their voices as though this was in doubt, and this reawakening is a miracle.

Blackbirds lead the dawn chorus. The robin's song is by turns sharp and serene, the dunnock's sweetly chatty. Song thrushes select detailed phrases. The chaffinch's song is strong and fruity. Collared doves coo, green woodpeckers laugh. Woodpigeons soar and flap over their territories.

Birds of prey rule the Gorge and it's a violent, noisy playground. Stiff-winged peregrines shoot out like arrows to defend their nest from other peregrines. The intruders persist, and lunging, screaming battles are fought above the river and woods. Ravens fly upside down provocatively. Peregrines dive at them, and at the buzzards that fan across from Leigh Woods. Sparrowhawks and kestrels scatter the jackdaws.

Birds fly in pairs. Male blackbirds are in their breeding plumage – smart black feathers with yellow beaks and eye rings that make them attractive to us, as well as to female blackbirds. Jackdaws preen their mates with infinite tenderness.

119

Arrivals! Swallows pass through the Gorge. I hear the rapid, bubbly notes of the blackcap above the Gully. Chiffchaffs, back from Africa, sing with enthusiasm even in this icy wind: these are male birds, arriving before the females to establish their territories.

Most redwings have left for Scandinavia.

All manner of violets flower in Fairyland, sweet and dog, purple, blue, white and red. Alexanders flower around shrub islands, and it's worth looking in the grass for the blue flowers of Buxbaum's speedwell.

Horse chestnut buds open, unpacking flower spikes from pleated leaves that daily become more emerald. Ash flower buds open, too, and at first the clusters look like loganberries. Several hawthorns are in leaf, as are small sycamores. The green tips of spindle are like lighted tapers. Blackthorn blossom begins.

A brimstone butterfly, looking like a flying primrose, journeys over the Dumps.

Hedgehogs are coming out of hibernation, and fox cubs are born.

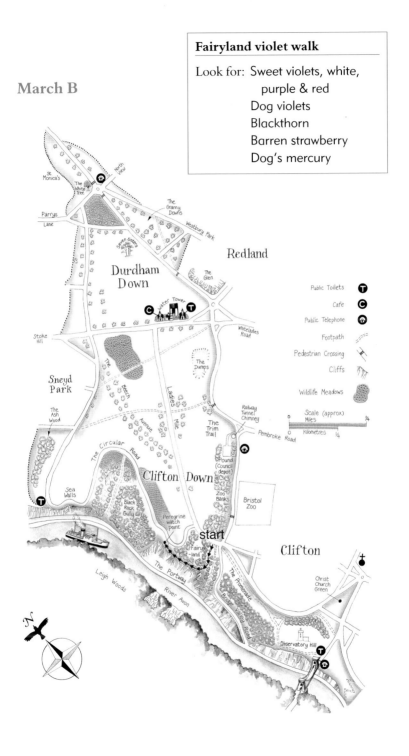

March B

Fairyland violet walk

Look for: Sweet violets, white,
purple & red
Dog violets
Blackthorn
Barren strawberry
Dog's mercury

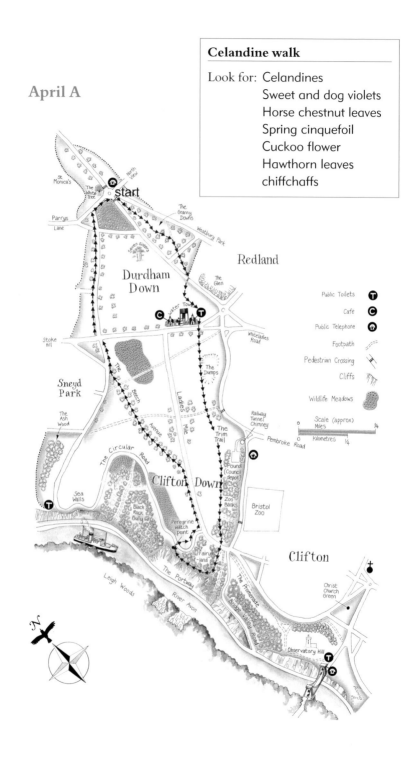

April A

Celandine walk

Look for: Celandines
 Sweet and dog violets
 Horse chestnut leaves
 Spring cinquefoil
 Cuckoo flower
 Hawthorn leaves
 chiffchaffs

What to Look for in **April**

March winds and April showers
bring forth May flowers

As I pass Wills Hall, a conglomeration of bark and twig falls at my feet. A crow is sitting in the top branch of the horse chestnut, regarding his dropped nesting material with an expression of despair.

A pril and the greening of the land begins; yellow flowers sparkle, birds sing overtures and we search the skies for the return of the swifts. The stage is set for the greatest show on Earth.

Birds build nests. Crows stuff dead leaves and grass into their beaks; magpies fly with sticks in theirs. Blackbirds plunge into shrub islands, beaks full of dry grass. Blue tits collect feathers. Jackdaws glide around exhibiting nesting material before taking it to the nest. Song thrushes select thin twigs from the ground around silver birches.

Courtship continues. Groups of jays chase through the top branches of Fairyland, uttering guttural warblings. Now and then, the males turn sideways to the females and raise their body feathers and crests enticingly. Male magpies vibrate their wings. Two nuthatches hurtle through a nearby ash; the male spreads his tail feathers, lifts his head to the sun and sings rich, bell like notes.

Chiffchaffs call on the Zoo Banks and the Dumps. These little birds dance on the branches between calls. Wrens, as rust-red as autumn brambles, sing in vibrant bursts. Raven chicks hatch. Cormorants fly earnestly one way or the other.

A passing wheatear appears on Durdham Down– these white-rumped birds fly low and often perch awhile on a small rock in the turf.

Snow at dawn: a chiffchaff calls from a snow-covered ash; a crow fluffs his wings and showers in the feathery white turf; goldfinches court on the snowy branches of a hawthorn. An hour later, the snow has melted and the familiar details of spring return.

A willow warbler sings on a hawthorn in the Dumps and a red kite patrols Clifton Down. At last the first swifts soar into view!

This is the month of yellow flowers: celandines, primroses, cowslips, dandelions, spring cinquefoil, buttercups. Early morning sun spotlights lemon cowslips; Fairyland Glade is golden with celandines, and pink cuckoo flower blossoms nearby. Bluebells appear here, and on the Zoo Banks. Spring cinquefoil flowers around small rocks and on the bank of Observatory Hill. Wood anemones, often called *windflowers*, dance near Fountain Hill. Dog violets are scattered singly in the grass like lost jewels.

Alexanders dominate Observatory Hill: fortunately the smell is softened by the Gorge wallflowers.

Cuckoo-pint's purple or yellow flowerheads appear.

The sycamore is unpacking its leaves and flowers. Bronze oak buds burst, and I find a seven spot ladybird clinging to one. The ferny branches of the silver birch have dainty new leaves, and gold and red catkins. Fairyland paths are strewn with ash flowers ripped off by the gales. Horse chestnuts flower. On the promenade turf, there are hundreds of baby beech trees like huge clover leaves. The Granny Downs is dizzy with green.

Two small tortoiseshell butterflies fly past the water tower. Later, I watch a peacock butterfly on a dandelion in Fairyland, spellbound by the stardust sheen of its wings.

I count 305 pairs of mating worms in a small portion of a football field.

A weasel scuttles between shrub islands.

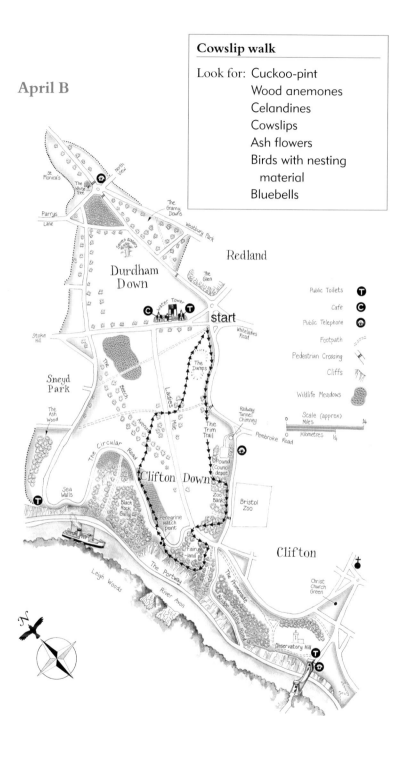

April B

Cowslip walk

Look for: Cuckoo-pint
Wood anemones
Celandines
Cowslips
Ash flowers
Birds with nesting
material
Bluebells

Redland

Durdham
Down

start

Sneyd
Park

Clifton Down

Clifton

Public Toilets **T**
Cafe **C**
Public Telephone
Footpath
Pedestrian Crossing
Cliffs
Wildlife Meadows

Scale (approx)
Miles
Kilometres

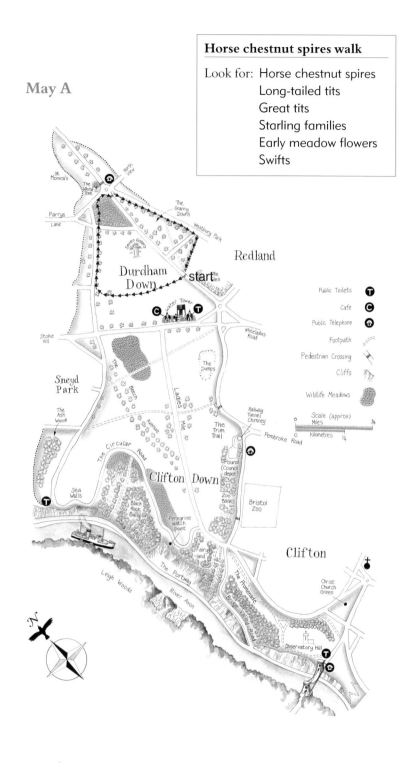

May A

Horse chestnut spires walk

Look for: Horse chestnut spires
Long-tailed tits
Great tits
Starling families
Early meadow flowers
Swifts

St Monica's

The White Tree

North View

The Granny Downs

Parrys Lane

Westbury Park

Seven Sisters

Redland

Durdham Down

start

The Glen

Public Toilets   **T**

Cafe   **C**

Public Telephone   ☎

Footpath

Pedestrian Crossing

Cliffs

Wildlife Meadows

Water Tower

C **T**

Whiteladies Road

Stoke Hill

The Dumps

Sneyd Park

The Beech

Ladies Mile

Railway Tunnel Chimney

Scale (approx)
Miles

Kilometres   ¼

The Ash Wood

Avenue

The Trim Trail

Pembroke Road

The Circular Road

Pound (Council depot)

☎

Clifton Down

Sea Walls

T

Black Rock Gully

Peregrine watch point

Zoo Banks

Bristol Zoo

Clifton

Fairy-land

Christ Church Green

The Portway

Leigh Woods

River Avon

The Promenade

Bridge Valley Road

Observatory Hill

T
☎

N

What to Look for in **May**

When the dew is on the grass
Rain will never come to pass

A sunny interlude in a wet morning. Six goldfinches
leave the shelter of a hawthorn on Clifton Down. They
fly first to the ground, and then each in turn jumps on
the stalks of dandelion clocks. Each rides their stalk as
it bends over, they secure the stalks to the ground with
their feet and pluck from the seed-head.
Now, a salmon-chested bullfinch leaves the same bush
and attempts this elegant procedure, only to give up in
a flurry.

May on the Downs is Bristol's glimpse of heaven on earth: a time
of blossom, fragrance, busy birds – and extremes of weather.
The air is electric with swifts screaming through the sky. Other
birds are feeding young and scolding anyone who ventures near the nests.
Walking across Clifton Down, I trigger the alarm calls of wrens, robins,
long-tailed tits, blackbirds and a blackcap. The latter is serious as blackcaps
rarely leave cover: best to apologise and move on quickly.

Blackcaps, dunnocks and the indefatigable chiffchaffs find time for a full
song, but otherwise birdsong between dawn and dusk comes in fragments.
Hawthorns, however, vibrate with the tinkle and wheeze of greenfinches.

In the Gorge cliffs, peregrines are on the nest. Raven chicks leave their
nest after much bravado and wing-flapping at the edge.

Speckly young starlings chase their parents, demanding food.

Families of long-tailed tits flit through the wooded areas around Clifton
Down, and in the Granny Downs. They cross from bush to bush in single

file, and demonstrate one of the greatest mysteries in bird watching – how do more long-tailed tits fly *out* of a bush than flew into it?

Flowers mark the journey from spring to summer. The month begins with golden carpets of buttercups and dandelions and ends with waves of meadow grass. Cow parsley flowers under hawthorns.

Of the spring flowers, cowslips are flowering around the Circular Road, and there are violets and a few bluebells around Fairyland Glade. In grassy areas, the yellow summer procession begins with rock-rose, yellow rattle, and bird's-foot-trefoil. Yellow herb bennet flowers in Fairyland.

Trees are at their full leaf finest. This is the month of fragrant white, or scentless pink hawthorn blossom, the spires of horse chestnut flowers, the creamy wayfaring tree blossom, the acid green whitebeam leaves – themselves as bright as blossom, and sharp-scented elder.

Elder is a traditional seasonal marker – the blossom heralding the summer, and the berries, the autumn.

The ash is still coming into leaf and there's a folk rhyme about the buds of the oak and the ash:

Oak before ash, barely a splash
Ash before oak, expect a soak

I have never seen ash before oak on the Bristol Downs and the *Woodland Trust* reports that the oak has been out first for 39 of the last 43 years.

A yellow crab spider waits for prey on creamy wayfaring blossom: this hunting spider camouflages itself by changing colour. If we see a butterfly clinging to a flower despite our close presence, it could mean that a crab spider is clasping it.

Butterflies, nevertheless, are plentiful. Common blues and orange-tip butterflies meander around the Dumps. Higher up on the holly itself, a holly blue's outer wings shine like silver. Speckled wood butterflies haunt the partly shaded areas of Fairyland.

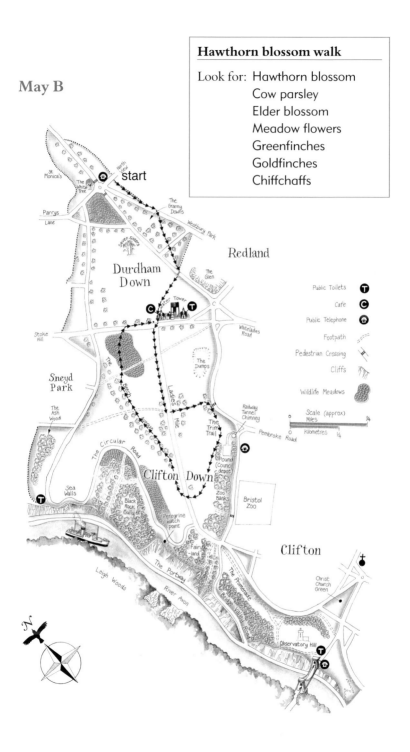

May B

Hawthorn blossom walk

Look for: Hawthorn blossom
Cow parsley
Elder blossom
Meadow flowers
Greenfinches
Goldfinches
Chiffchaffs

start

St Monica's
The White Tree
Parrys Lane
North Road
The Granny Downs
Westbury Park
Redland
Seven Sisters
Durdham Down
The Glen
Water Tower
Stoke Hill
Whiteladies Road
Sneyd Park
The Dumps
The Ash Wood
The Beeches
Ladies Mile
Railway Tunnel Chimney
The Trim Trail
Pembroke Road
The Circular Road
Clifton Down
Sea Walls
Black Rock Gully
Peregrine watch point
Pound (Council) depot
Zoo Banks
Bristol Zoo
Fairy land
Clifton
The Portway
Leigh Woods
River Avon
Bridge Valley Road
The Promenade
Christ Church Green
Observatory Hill

Public Toilets 🅣
Cafe 🅒
Public Telephone ☎
Footpath
Pedestrian Crossing
Cliffs
Wildlife Meadows

Scale (approx)
Miles
0   ¼
0   Kilometres   ¼

N

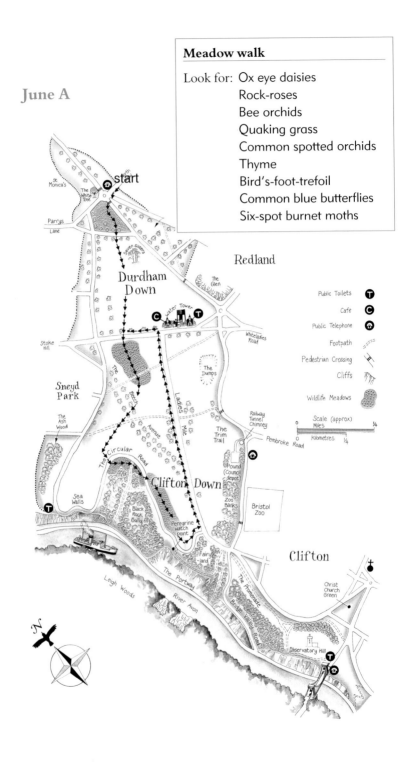

June A

Meadow walk

Look for: Ox eye daisies
Rock-roses
Bee orchids
Quaking grass
Common spotted orchids
Thyme
Bird's-foot-trefoil
Common blue butterflies
Six-spot burnet moths

start

St Monica's
The White Tree

Parrys Lane

Seven Sisters

Redland

The Glen

Durdham Down

Water Tower

Stoke Hill

Wheeladies Road

The Dumps

Sneyd Park

The Ash Wood

Railway Tunnel Chimney

The Trim Trail

Avenue

Ladies Mile

Pembroke Road

The Circular Road

Pound (Council depot)

Clifton Down

Zoo Banks

Bristol Zoo

Sea Walls

Black Rock Gully

Peregrine watch point

Fairyland

Clifton

Leigh Woods

River Avon

The Portway

Bridge Valley Road

The Promenade

Christ Church Green

Observatory Hill

Public Toilets **T**

Cafe **C**

Public Telephone

Footpath

Pedestrian Crossing

Cliffs

Wildlife Meadows

Scale (approx)
Miles   ¼
Kilometres   ¼

N

What to Look for in **June**

When ditch and pond offend the nose
Then look for rain and stormy blows

In a tangle of rosebush and hawthorn, three baby
long-tailed tits and two scruffy young blue tits fluff and
preen on the same branch, pressed close together.
Now a baby wren pushes into the middle of the row.
One blue tit falls off, shakes itself, flies up to the branch
again, and regains a place. They huddle even closer to
accommodate the wren.

June on the Downs is the meadow month: grasses ripple, orchids bloom, dragonflies patrol, butterflies settle. Our meadows are as exciting as any I know.

Bird activity centres on the shrub islands – those tangles of hawthorn, ivy, bramble, elder, wild rose, yew and traveller's-joy that are the wildlife havens of the Downs. Stand near an island and hear baby birds calling to be fed. Parent blue tits venture to the outer branches and scruffy, yellow babies follow them.

Singing is patchy – reliably wren and the chaffinch, greenfinch and chiffchaff: snatches of blackcap, robin, blackbird and song thrush. Increasingly, though, there are periods of silence.

In the Gorge cliffs, young peregrines fledge and the family begins its spectacular flying displays: watchers gather to see these magnificent hunting birds soar, circle and dive.

On Durdham Down, young mistle thrushes, their chests like spotted dick puddings, congregate and take turns to step a few paces at a time.

The meadows are embroidered with flowers: thyme, kidney vetch, yellow rattle, quaking grass, ox eye daisies, rock-roses, bladder campion, bird's-foot-trefoil, pink common spotted orchids, bee and sometimes wasp and pyramidal orchids.

In the short turf there's white and red clover, purple self-heal, buttercups and daisies.

Red valerian grows in and around the Sea Walls.

Trees are darker, leaves thicker. Elm seeds are like orange flying saucers in the grass and conker cases and beech nut cases are prominent now. Clifton Down is rich with elder and wild rose. I believe that the silky petals of the wild rose have a faint rosy perfume, although perhaps my brain is playing tricks.

At the end of this month the limes begin to blossom, and the cream flowers release the headiest fragrance on earth.

Butterflies fly around the meadows: marbled whites, meadow browns, and ringlets. The latter have white-centred eye-spots on the underside.

Six-spot burnet moths cling to grass stems. The wings of these day-flying moths resemble wizards' cloaks – each forewing has six large red spots on a black, metallic ground. On the Downs, they visit scabious and knapweed, and I have also seen them on common spotted orchids.

Above the White Tree meadow on sunny afternoons, emperor dragonflies chase each other like miniature fighter planes.

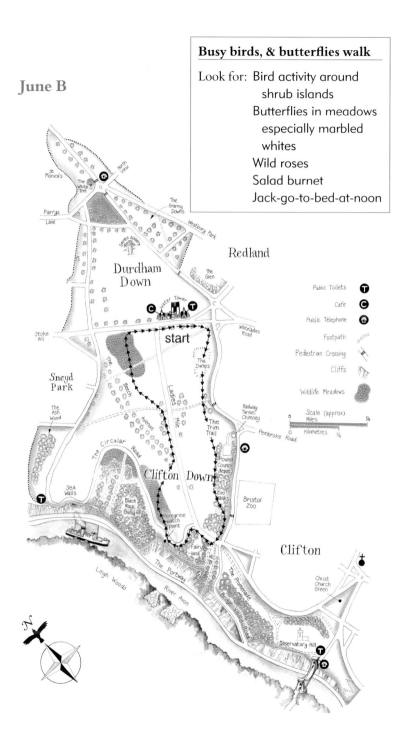

June B

Busy birds, & butterflies walk

Look for: Bird activity around
shrub islands
Butterflies in meadows
especially marbled
whites
Wild roses
Salad burnet
Jack-go-to-bed-at-noon

St. Monica's
North View
The White Tree
Parrys Lane
The Granny Downs
Westbury Park
Seven Sisters
Redland
Durdham Down
The Glen
Water Tower
start
Whiteladies Road
Stoke Hill
The Dumps
The Beach
Ladies Mile
Sneyd Park
The Ash Wood
The Avenue
Railway Tunnel Chimney
The Trim Trail
Pembroke Road
The Circular Road
Pound Council depot
Clifton Down
Zoo Banks
Bristol Zoo
Sea Walls
Black Rock Gully
Peregrine watch point
Fairy-land
Clifton
The Portway
Leigh Woods
River Avon
The Promenade
Suspension Bridge
Bridge Valley Road
Christ Church Green
Observatory Hill

Public Toilets
Cafe
Public Telephone
Footpath
Pedestrian Crossing
Cliffs
Wildlife Meadows
Scale (approx)
Miles
Kilometres

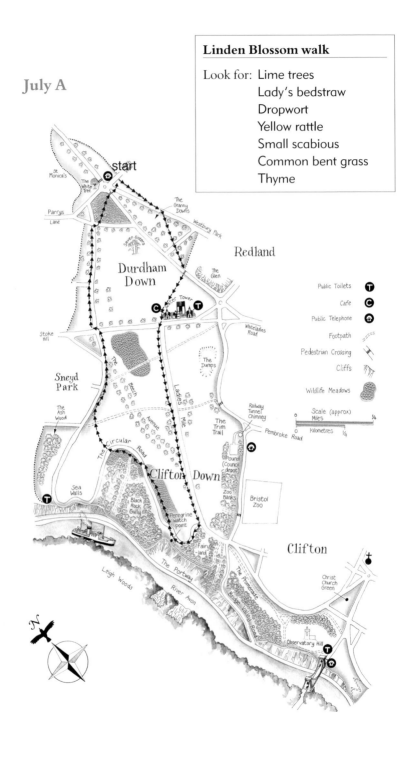

July A

Linden Blossom walk

Look for: Lime trees
Lady's bedstraw
Dropwort
Yellow rattle
Small scabious
Common bent grass
Thyme

start

St. Monica's

The White Tree

Parrys Lane

The Granny Downs

Westbury Park

Redland

Seven Sisters

Durdham Down

The Glen

Water Tower

Whiteladies Road

Stoke Hill

Sneyd Park

The Dumps

The Ash Wood

The Beech Avenue

Ladies Mile

Railway Tunnel Chimney

The Trim Trail

Pembroke Road

The Circular Road

Pound (Council depot)

Clifton Down

Zoo Banks

Bristol Zoo

Sea Walls

Black Rock Gully

Peregrine watch point

Fairy land

Clifton

Leigh Woods

River Avon

The Portway

Observatory Hill

The Promenade

Bridge Valley Road

Christ Church Green

Public Toilets	**T**
Cafe	**C**
Public Telephone	**☎**
Footpath	
Pedestrian Crossing	
Cliffs	
Wildlife Meadows	

Scale (approx)
Miles
0 ¼
0 ¼
Kilometres

N

What to Look for in **July**

When black slugs on the path you see
Then on the morrow, rain will be

A squadron of three peregrines suddenly rears up
from the Gorge and flies in line towards the rooks
of the Ash Wood. One by one they soar up and then
turn downwards, wings tight against their bodies like
arrowheads. They each dive at their selected rook,
veering away from it at the last second, then soar back
over the Gorge, flipping over in a victory roll.

July is the month of beautiful surprises; linden (lime tree) blossom;
exquisite dropwort; peregrine air shows; and, if the weather is moody,
rainbows, and butterflies clinging to long grass.

Birds are busy with families, or moulting. Apart from contact calls, they
are mostly silent although dunnocks and blackcaps sing in snatches. The
chiffchaff sings but with diminishing stamina.

Goldfinch families fly around the upper branches of shrub islands,
wrens weave through the lower parts leading tiny young, and juvenile
chiffchaffs tumble through the branches of small trees. Thin squeaks of
goldcrests can be heard in yew canopies.

Blackbirds are still feeding their young at the base of shrub islands,
poking food into the mouths of youngsters hidden inside.

Chattering families of long-tailed tits flit from tree to tree. Green
woodpeckers can sometimes be observed with two or three young
hopping behind in military formation. Swifts form screaming parties and
hurtle around the Downs and the streets nearby.

The peregrine falcon family race and glide in the wind, the juveniles
flying with increasing panache.

A kestrel hovers above the Dumps, then soars away like a flying crossbow. At Peregrine Watch Point, a sparrowhawk scatters the jackdaws.

Flowers flourish in the meadows. Lady's bedstraw forms yellow patches: once it was used to stuff mattresses, though I doubt if mattresses were as thick as they are now. Thyme spreads, white fairy flax twinkles, yellow-starred agrimony soars, lilac scabious towers. Common bent grass swirls like purple currents.

Near the Worrall Road crossing, there's a display of rosebay willowherb and meadow cranesbill. In the Circular Road meadows, there are coronets of dropwort, its buds coral and its flowers pearly. Black knapweed with its pink, geometric flowers appears in the meadows, and in the Circular Road meadows – yellowwort, and bubble-gum pink centaury.

Jack-go-to-bed-at-noon flowers in the long grass: around noon the flowers shut! These flowers become enormous dandelion clocks, giving rise to their other name – *goat's beard*.

Hedge bindweed, bramble and traveller's joy blossom on shrub islands, and sometimes, this month, the Downs is white with clover.

Trees flounce and roar in the high winds of July. The fragrance of nectar-rich linden blossom floods the air, swarming with bees. By the end of July, the blossoms have become hard seeds, but the fragrance lingers as though the air is reluctant to let go of something so beautiful.

Hawthorn berries are blushed with coral, and, deceptively, conker cases look ready to fall. Holly berries are fat and green.

Butterflies cling to meadow grass when it's too cold and wet for them to fly: they need the sun's warmth to bring their wing muscles to working temperature.

When the sun shines, common blue butterflies open into velvet bows, marbled whites flip their wings apart but continue to cling, and meadow brown butterflies are the first to leave the grass. Meadow grasshoppers scatter as I walk.

Fungi turns up when conditions are right (wet and warm) and hundreds of fairies' bonnets appear under a horse chestnut in the Granny Downs – tiers of tiny mushrooms.

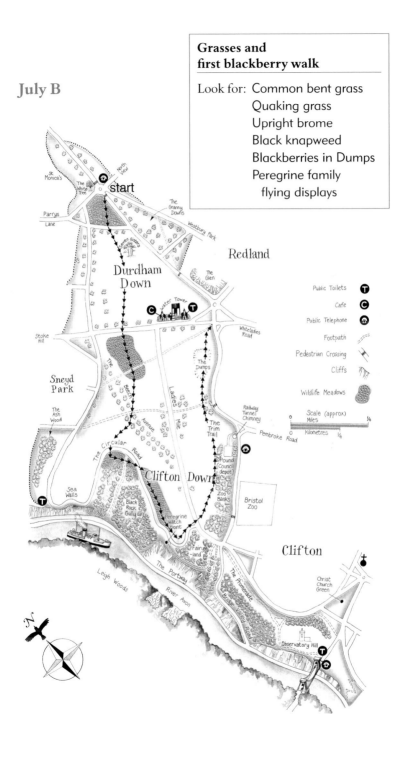

July B

Grasses and first blackberry walk

Look for: Common bent grass
Quaking grass
Upright brome
Black knapweed
Blackberries in Dumps
Peregrine family
flying displays

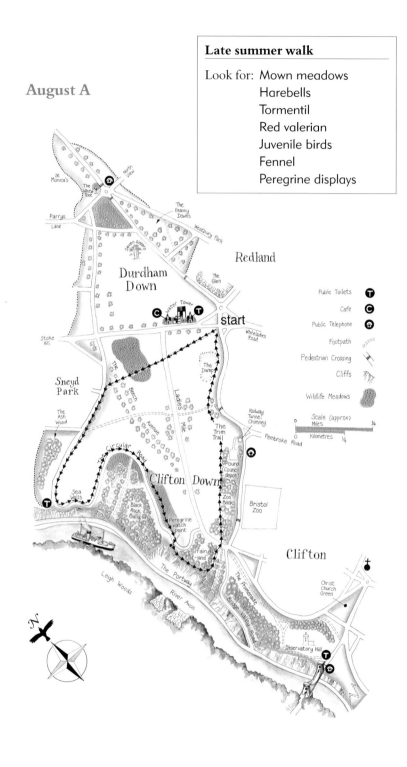

August A

Late summer walk

Look for: Mown meadows
Harebells
Tormentil
Red valerian
Juvenile birds
Fennel
Peregrine displays

Redland

St.
Monica's
The
White
Tree
North View

Parrys
Lane
The
Granny
Downs
Westbury Park

Seven Sisters

Durdham
Down

The
Glen

Water Tower

start

Whiteladies
Road

Stoke
Hill

The
Dump

Sneyd
Park

The
Ash
Wood

Beech

Ladies Mile

Avenue

Railway
Tunnel
Chimney

Pembroke Road

The
Trim
Trail

The Circular Road

Sea
Walls

Black
Rock
Gully

Peregrine
watch
point

Pound
Council
depot

Zoo
Banks

Bristol
Zoo

Clifton Down

Fairy-
land

Clifton

Legh Woods

River Avon

The Portway

The Promenade

Bridge Valley Road

Christ
Church
Green

Observatory Hill

Public Toilets **T**

Cafe **C**

Public Telephone

Footpath

Pedestrian Crossing

Cliffs

Wildlife Meadows

Scale (approx)
Miles   ¼
Kilometres   ¼

N

What to Look for in **August**

When the leaves show their undersides
Be very sure that rain betides

Not expecting to hear birdsong and registering that
even the chiffchaffs were silent, I was surprised to hear a
babbling of music coming from a shrub island. I waited
until the sun came from behind a cloud and shone a
searchlight into the island. It was a robin, at the end of
his moult, practising his autumn sub-song.

A ugust holds the seasons in balance. The mown meadows reflect
the rhythm of the countryside, and give us the scent of hay. But the
vistas seem empty and hushed, and the trees dark. Yet for newly fledged
birds, as for children, August is playtime.

Birds dash between shrub islands, the newly fledged flying with excited
energy. Young goldfinches (chests silver in the sun) flitter with greenfinches
and baby great tits, and then perch high up and survey the world. Tiny
wrens weave around the base of shrub islands and then fly under the radar
from one island to another, vibrating like conker-red moths.

Young blackbirds practise landing skills in the hawthorns. Juvenile jays
practise theirs in ashes and sycamores. Baby magpies squawk and flap.
A fluffed-up juvenile kestrel sits on an ash and stares at the grass: young
long-tailed tits dance through the shade behind him.

Fledged green woodpeckers guffaw experimentally, and juvenile rooks
and crows loiter around their parents, hoping to be fed.

Freed of the harassment of their young, starlings flock, wheel, and then
gather to gossip in the trees lining Stoke Road.

Robins return from their moult at the end of this month, and pull at our heartstrings with their subdued autumn sub-song. The swifts leave in August: we remember them, look up, but the skies are empty.

Flowers are surprisingly plentiful. Harebells flower again after the mowing, and the mats of yellow tormentil often escape the blades. This is a purple month – musk thistle, black knapweed, woody nightshade and the striped purple and green field garlic. The loveliest of willowherbs, greater willowherb, has widened its range, and on both sides of Ladies Mile there are patches of its cherry pink.

In the Dumps, there are mustard yellow flowers on fennel.

Autumn lady's tresses orchids are flowering in a meadow near the Circular Road but can be maddeningly hard to find. These frosty little orchids have the distinction of being featured in Ian Fleming's *On Her Majesty's Secret Service*. The Head of the Secret Service (M) paints them, and sings their praises to James Bond as being proper orchids, as opposed to the tropical varieties:

> *Now that – M waved at the meagre little bloom in the tooth-glass – that's the real thing. That's an Autumn Lady's-tresses – Spiranthes spiralis.*

Trees are dark-leaved and some leaves are rusty. Sycamore keys are blushed with coral, conkers fatter and beech cases are rough and brown.

Lime seeds spiral elegantly to the ground where the brown wings give an illusion of an early autumn. Clumps of ash keys hang down like dirty dishcloths. There are tight-fisted little acorns on the holm oaks.

Blackberries are at their best at the end of this month. Hawthorn berries have turned from coral to a soft red, and elder berries are purple. At the foot of shrubs, scarlet cuckoo-pint berries take us by surprise.

Butterflies feast on blackberries and we can get close to red admirals. While looking at these, I am sometimes rewarded with a glimpse of the small copper butterfly feeding on a remaining bramble flower. Meadow brown butterflies sun themselves on the cut hay.

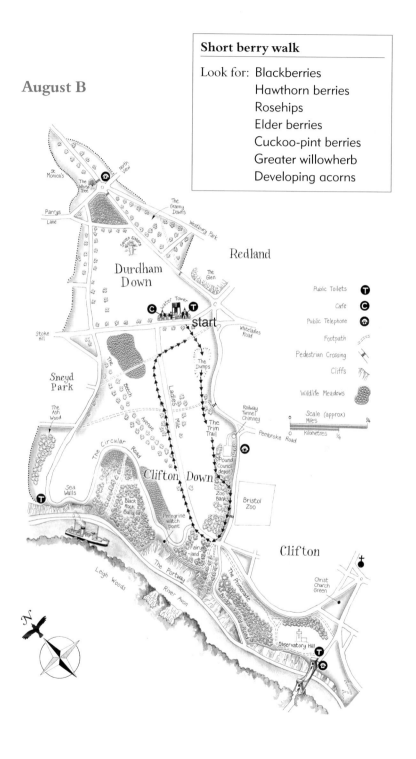

August B

Short berry walk

Look for: Blackberries
Hawthorn berries
Rosehips
Elder berries
Cuckoo-pint berries
Greater willowherb
Developing acorns

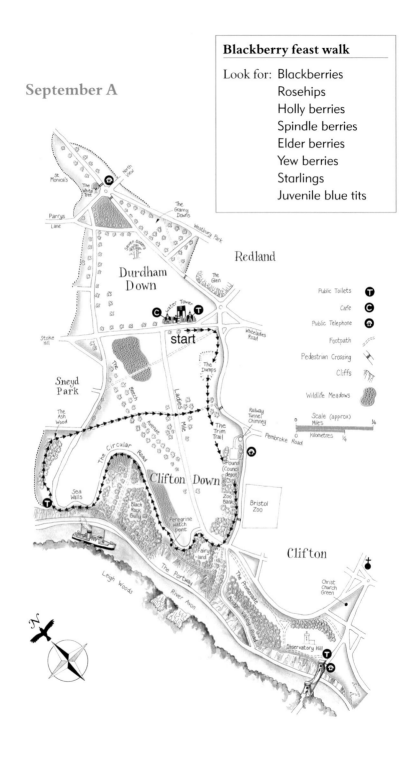

September A

Blackberry feast walk

Look for: Blackberries
Rosehips
Holly berries
Spindle berries
Elder berries
Yew berries
Starlings
Juvenile blue tits

What to Look for in **September**

When the clouds appear like rocks and towers
The earth's refreshed by frequent showers

9th September – Clifton Down. Black skies and a rainbow.
The rainbow ends in a hawthorn and the crow on top is
bathed in colour.

In September the slow gilding of the land begins. The Downs is ruby-rich with berries, and the plumed seeds of wild clematis surf the shrub islands.

Many juvenile birds have dispersed and others engage in repetitive behaviour. I observe a young magpie jump on and off a wooden seat, and later, I watch a juvenile pied wagtail encircling a lamppost.

Four mallards fly up the Gorge to the Suspension bridge, turn back, and then repeat this performance.

Shrub islands are magicians' hats; dozens of long-tailed tits burst out of them in single file. Sometimes, a juvenile blue tit, the colour of mimosa, hesitates at the end of the branch, and then launches off to join them. In early autumn, it's usually a single blue tit (or great tit) that joins the long-tailed circus. Later, the bird congregations are a mixture of blue tits, coal tits, treecreepers, long-tailed tits, chaffinches, great tits and sometimes a nuthatch.

Alarm calls erupt from shrub islands as I pass –juvenile robins and wrens are practising their protests.

Chiffchaffs sing in short bursts: they return to Africa shortly.

Sometimes winter thrushes (fieldfares and redwings) fly over the Downs, but it's too early for them to settle here.

Peregrines drive their young away by stooping and pursuit. Starlings come from all directions to gossip in the giant ash on Clifton Down.

Flowers dwindle, though there are latecomers. Purple and yellow woody nightshade lurks in the Dumps, and some of the berries are green. Woody nightshade is often mistaken for deadly nightshade: this does not grow on the Downs although for years there was a splendid bush near the Zoo. Soap-smelling hedge bedstraw is still unfolding in the Dumps, and wild carrot with its single red flower in the middle, blossoms in Fairyland.

Hoary plantain's fragrant white stamens look fresh, and parents still show children how to fire ribwort plantain heads.

Clumps of rosebay willowherb's feathery seeds detach and drift– these are widely called *fairies* because they shine like rainbows in the sunlight.

Trees and berries lead the autumn transformation. The horse chestnuts are the first to golden and once started, this change is rapid. Now at last, ripe conkers begin to fall. Lime seeds spiral down and there are as many on the ground as on the trees. Beeches are also becoming golden and the woody cases opening to release tasty little nuts. Many of these cases remain on the branches as four-petalled wooden flowers.

A smattering of the leaves on the birches and limes has turned to yellow.

Elder is heavy with ripe berries and all over the Downs, woodpigeons are making fools of themselves by toppling off the branches in an attempt to eat them.

Sycamore wings are brown and papery and many have fallen. It's amusing to walk along Ladies Mile looking at the seeds on the pavement as a guide to the trees above.

Spindle berries are apple blossom pink, and wild rose haws all shades of orange. The mossy-cupped acorns of sessile oaks are well developed and some are already brown.

Strands of black bryony berries droop over shrub islands.

Yew berries are translucent in the sun.

Garden cross spiders have spun webs on blackberry bushes and vibrate them when I pick a blackberry nearby.

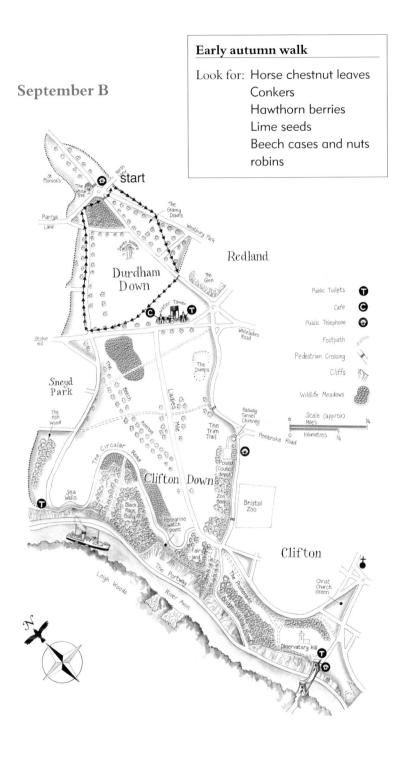

September B

Early autumn walk

Look for: Horse chestnut leaves
Conkers
Hawthorn berries
Lime seeds
Beech cases and nuts
robins

start

St. Monica's
The White Tree
North Side
The Granny Downs
Parrys Lane
Westbury Park
Seven Sisters
Redland
Durdham Down
The Glen
Water Tower
Whiteladies Road
Stoke Hill
The Dumps
Sneyd Park
The Ash Wood
Beech Avenue
Ladies Mile
Railway Tunnel Chimney
The Trim Trail
Pembroke Road
The Circular Road
Pound (Council depot)
Clifton Down
Sea Walls
Black Rock Gully
Zoo Banks
Bristol Zoo
Peregine Watch point
Fairy land
Clifton
The Portway
Leigh Woods
River Avon
Bridge Valley Road
The Promenade
Christ Church Green
Observatory Hill

Public Toilets   **T**
Cafe   **C**
Public Telephone   ☎
Footpath
Pedestrian Crossing
Cliffs
Wildlife Meadows

Scale (approx)
Miles   ¼
Kilometres   ¼

N

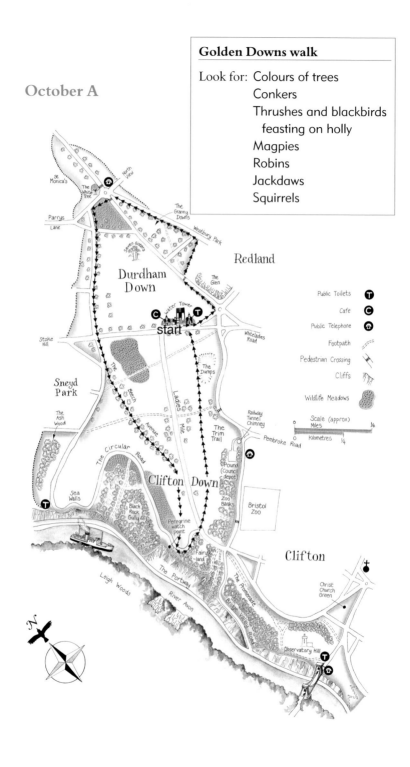

October A

Redland

Durdham
Down

start

Stoke
Hill

Sneyd
Park

The
Ash
Wood

Clifton Down

Clifton

Sea
Walls

Black
Rock
Gully

Peregrine
watch
point

Fairy-
land

Bristol
Zoo

Zoo
Banks

Pembroke Road

Railway
Tunnel
Chimney

The Trim
Trail

The Dumps

Whiteladies
Road

The Glen

Westbury Park

The Granny
Downs

Parrys
Lane

St.
Monica's

The
White
Tree

North
View

Seven Sisters

Water Tower

Leigh Woods

River Avon

The Portway

The Promenade

Bridge Valley Road

Christ
Church
Green

Observatory Hill

Pound
(Council
depot)

The Circular Road

The Avenue

Ladies Mile

The Beech

Public Toilets
Cafe
Public Telephone
Footpath
Pedestrian Crossing
Cliffs
Wildlife Meadows

Scale (approx)
Miles
Kilometres
¼

N

What to Look for in **October**

When you see gossamer flying
Be sure the air is drying

Early morning on Clifton Down. Suddenly there's a powerful vibration in the air and two dog walkers check their phones to see if they are responsible. The noise grows to UFO proportions. I look up and see a whooper swan low-flying towards Stoke Bishop.

Octctober and we walk towards the heart of autumn. Trees parade their coats of many colours against turbulent grey skies. Leaves drift down to become golden shadows under golden trees, and the slightest sunbeam sets the landscape on fire. Then suddenly, the first frosts conjure an even more mysterious landscape…

Birds feast on nuts and berries. Now that the elder berries have dwindled, the turf around the beeches is encircled with woodpigeons feeding on nuts. Blackbirds and song thrushes gorge holly berries. Jays make a business of flying backwards and forwards across the Gorge, selecting acorns from Leigh Woods to bury on the Downs, and screeching with high-minded importance.

Robins are the dominant singers, establishing and defending territories. When the sun shines, there are bursts of wren song, a few chiffchaff repetitions, a couple of great tit calls, bullfinch *mews*, chaffinch *pinks*, and the twinkling of high-flying goldfinches.

Early in the month, house martins and swallows swoop across Clifton Down, heading south.

Starlings sing in the rain. Sometimes, during downpours and buffeting winds, hundreds of starlings crowd the giant ash on Clifton Down. Some sing melodies above the whistles and tweets of others. Later, they float to the ground in ones and twos like the leaves falling around them.

Magpies strut, shout and show off their tails. Jackdaws flap about in large groups over Clifton Down and the Gorge: a sharp wind brings them together in play with rooks, magpies and woodpigeons. The latter dash to be in the thick of bird action, like playground children.

Groups of redwings and fieldfares fill the sky: we can hear their contact calls as they fly over in the night. When there is frost, the rising sun paints the gulls pink, and the flying redwings a rich red.

Winter's breath is in the wind, and robins fluff up against the cold.

Flowers surprise us. There's red and white clover, a few dandelions and, at the beginning of the month, a couple of harebells on the Zoo banks. Yellow gorse lights up the sides of the Gorge.

Ivy flowers appear and these offer the last nectar of the year.

Trees: Horse chestnuts are auburn, illuminated from within. Beneath them, conkers crowd like cobblestones, and the vibration from lorries brings more crashing down. The red of conkers varies from tree to tree and the watermark on each conker is unique: this is best seen in sunlight when the conker case is first opened. Squirrels feed on conkers and pelt across roads carrying them in their mouths.

The Promenade of beeches is gilding, and in morning mist, the leaves are like pebbles under water. Limes and plane trees are increasingly yellow, sycamores blush pink and oaks return to the bronze they wore in the spring. As canopies thin, dark branches are revealed again.

The leaves of spindle bushes are yellow and green, and the pink berries now show orange flesh in the middle.

There is an uplifting show of holly berries on Clifton down, also rosehips, and hawthorn berries are a dull red, and soft to touch.

Blackberries are mouldy, though one or two might be worth the risk.

Fungi occur. In particular, sixty-three shaggy ink caps (lawyers' wigs) near a roadside on the Granny Downs in all stages from furled beginnings to slop. I also find the small buttercup-yellow, hat-like *Bolbitius vitellinus* in the Clifton Down turf.

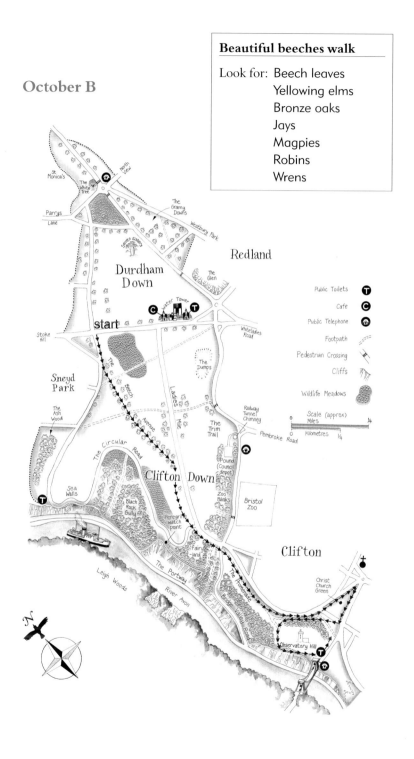

October B

Beautiful beeches walk

Look for: Beech leaves
Yellowing elms
Bronze oaks
Jays
Magpies
Robins
Wrens

Redland

Durdham
Down

start

Sneyd
Park

The Ash
Wood

Stoke
Hill

The Circular Road

Sea
Walls

Black
Rock
Gully

Clifton Down

Peregrine
watch
point

Fairy-
land

The
Dumps

Ladies' Mile

The
Beech
Avenue

Whiteladies
Road

The
Glen

The
Granny
Downs

Westbury Park

Seven Sisters

St.
Monica's

The
White
Tree

North
View

Parrys
Lane

Water Tower

Railway
Tunnel
Chimney

The
Trim
Trail

Pembroke Road

Pound
(Council
depot)

Zoo
Banks

Bristol
Zoo

Clifton

Christ
Church
Green

The Portway

River Avon

Leigh Woods

The Promenade

Bridge Valley Road

Observatory Hill

Public Toilets T

Cafe C

Public Telephone

Footpath

Pedestrian Crossing

Cliffs

Wildlife Meadows

Scale (approx)
Miles   ¼
Kilometres   ¼

N

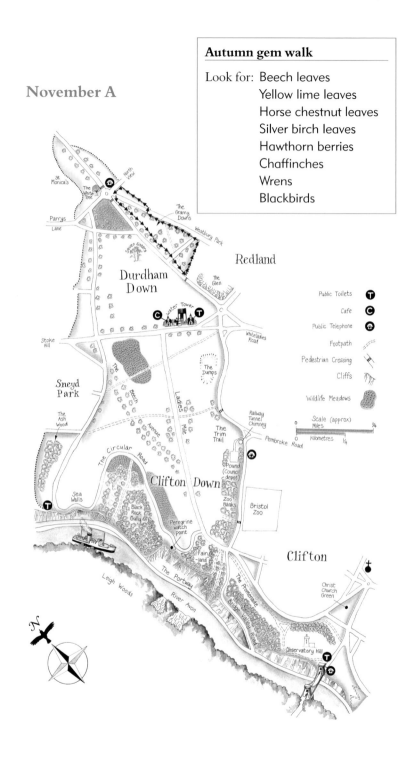

November A

Autumn gem walk

Look for: Beech leaves
Yellow lime leaves
Horse chestnut leaves
Silver birch leaves
Hawthorn berries
Chaffinches
Wrens
Blackbirds

St. Monica's
North View
The White Tree
Parrys Lane
The Granny Downs
Westbury Park
Redland
Seven Sisters
Durdham Down
The Glen
Water Tower
Stoke Hill
Whiteladies Road
The Dumps
Sneyd Park
The Beech
The Ash Wood
Ladies Mile
Railway Tunnel Chimney
The Trim Trail
Pembroke Road
The Circular Road
Avenue
Clifton Down
Pound (Council depot)
Zoo Banks
Bristol Zoo
Sea Walls
Black Rock Gully
Peregrine watch point
Fairy-land
Clifton
Christ Church Green
The Portway
Legh Woods
River Avon
The Promenade
Bridge Valley Road
Observatory Hill

Public Toilets   **T**
Cafe   **C**
Public Telephone
Footpath
Pedestrian Crossing
Cliffs
Wildlife Meadows

Scale (approx)
Miles
0   1/4
Kilometres
0   1/4

N

What to Look for in **November**

Seagull, seagull, sit on the sand
It's never good weather when you're on the land

Frost before sunrise. Dozens of redwings and a couple of fieldfares above Clifton Down. The scarlet sun rises above the horizon and for the couple of minutes before it yellows, birds dash about as though they've absorbed its energy. Redwings leave the holly and the hawthorns, and fly with the smaller birds in this sunrise ballet. Now bullfinches, chaffinches, great tits and goldfinches weave amongst the redwing arrivals. Our native thrushes – song and mistle – hold themselves aloof, and blackbirds are cautious.

November holds the fiery soul of autumn, and the birth of winter. Winds strip brittle-leaved trees, and galvanise the flying of jackdaws. Redwings bring new music. Darkness hovers. Our world changes.

Gulls stream along the Avon and over the Downs. When they are not quarrelling among themselves, black-headed gulls supervise and chivvy the starlings that feed with them on the turf.

Birds ride the wind: rooks tumble; pied wagtails bounce sideways in flight; jackdaws plunge into the Gorge and rocket up again. Peregrines and kestrels soar, hover, and dive. On these windy fly-about mornings, gulls chase crows, crows chase buzzards, and the peregrines chase anything within range.

Small birds huddle in shrubs, or make short flights in wooded areas.

Trees are radiant, lit from within. The Promenade of beeches is a path through a planet not quite our own.

The kerfuffle of blue tits in the canopies causes lime leaves to fall, as do the secretive treetop explorations of coal tits.

Piles of brown leaves collect under ash trees. Long-tailed tits tumble through the branches and release more leaves to clatter down: the ash leaf is the noisiest of the falling leaves.

Wych elms are lemon in the fragile sunlight. Spindle bushes glow with sunset colours.

In the rushing winds, horse chestnuts toss their auburn heads and roar, and dry leaves skip along the roads like excited children. Sunbeams kindle the embers of beeches, and against a dark sky, fleeting rainbows begin and end in the clouds.

Silver birches are the last to turn and their golden shimmer means that, soon, autumn's light will be out.

Flowers crop up here and there. A few daisies, the odd buttercup and a smattering of autumn hawkbit – a small dandelion with red stripes on the underside of the petals.

Fungi are interesting. The waxy yellow and red waxcap toadstools crop up in grassy areas, and earth star fungi occur in Fairyland and on the Zoo Banks. There is a sinister collection of sickly green death cap fungus close to an oak in a secluded part of the Zoo Banks: this is one of our most deadly fungi.

Badgers are busy at night; there are holes made by their snuffling for food under a holm oak on the Zoo Banks, and paths through the wet grass, indicating their nocturnal journeys. Squirrels frolic in this land of plenty, chasing up and around trees, bounding across the roads, and sometimes sitting and scolding with jay-like harshness.

Fairyland is enchanting and the path along the Gorge is waymarked by yew, holly and spindle berries. Yellow-leaved field maple lights the woodland, and little furry creatures (probably wood mice or bank voles) scuttle beneath fallen, crackling leaves. There's sunshine yellow gorse at the Gorge edge, the scent of sweet violet leaves, and an earthstar fungus beside the path.

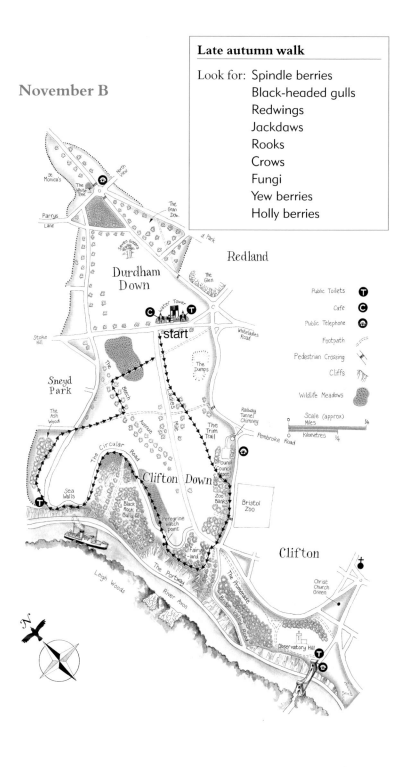

November B

Late autumn walk

Look for: Spindle berries
Black-headed gulls
Redwings
Jackdaws
Rooks
Crows
Fungi
Yew berries
Holly berries

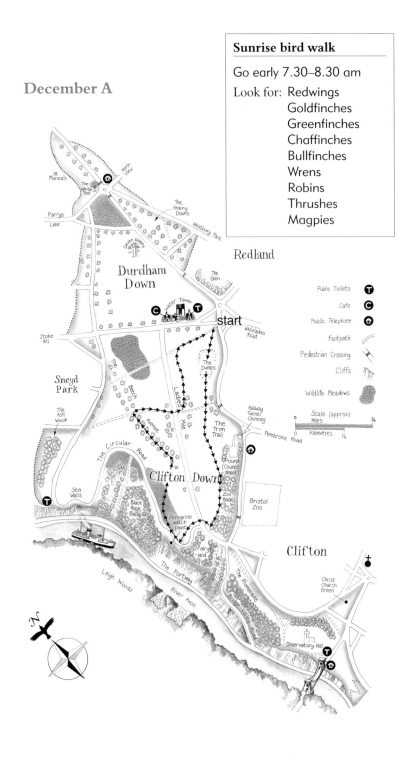

December A

Sunrise bird walk

Go early 7.30–8.30 am

Look for: Redwings
            Goldfinches
            Greenfinches
            Chaffinches
            Bullfinches
            Wrens
            Robins
            Thrushes
            Magpies

St Monica's

North View

The White Tree

The Granny Downs

Parrys Lane

Westbury Park

Seven Sisters

Redland

Durdham Down

The Glen

Water Tower

start

Whiteladies Road

Stoke Hill

The Beach

Sneyd Park

Ladies Mile

The Dumps

The Ash Wood

Avenue

Railway Tunnel Chimney

Pembroke Road

The Trim Trail

The Circular Road

Clifton Down

Pound (Council depot)

Sea Walls

Black Rock Gully

Peregrine watch point

Zoo Banks

Bristol Zoo

Fairy-land

Clifton

The Portway

Leigh Woods

River Avon

The Promenade

Bridge Valley Road

Christ Church Green

Observatory Hill

Public Toilets   **T**

Cafe   **C**

Public Telephone   **☎**

Footpath

Pedestrian Crossing

Cliffs

Wildlife Meadows

Scale (approx)
Miles   ¼
Kilometres   ¼

N

What to Look for in **December**

*When rooks fly sporting high in air
It shows that windy storms are near*

A dark morning with gauntlets of rain and a forecast of
70 mph gales. Nothing much to see today, I tell myself,
just a few black-headed gulls wading along the shores
of big puddles on Durdham Down. But here come the
starlings in a swirling corps de ballet. A dozen or so
of them land in each puddle, stand side-by-side like a
chorus line and shower, sending up mists of spray over
each other. Now they exchange puddles, line up and
splash again!

December and the sun stirs the smouldering embers of autumn.
Silver birches briefly reach their golden finest, but most trees are
bare. The landscape is often flooded, and whipped by gales. Yet there's
beauty in the watercolours of winter, in the pencil tracery of branches, and
in the fluffed up vulnerability of birds.

When there's a frost, the dawn is opal and the clouds are apricot and
lilac. Sunlight is low and the turf a rich green with long shadows.

Rain floods the turf and black-headed gulls gather to harvest
worms surfacing from the sodden earth. Starlings feed with the gulls, and
the usual squabbling occurs. Often a gull takes exception to a particular
starling and chases it across the Downs. Now and then, all the starlings
take off, circle, regroup and fly back into the middle of the gull gang.

Birds venturing out between downpours are easily seen in leafless
trees, as are the remains of nests. Pied wagtails skim the turf, land and
wag on the tarmac areas of the Sea Walls. Song thrushes sing before

sunrise, alternating bubbling phrases with loud, clear calls: they are singing to claim territories. Large-eyed robins look for food in the gloom, woodpigeons fluff their feathers like duvets and sit in the elms. Wrens weave around brambles. Dunnocks mutter in hawthorns.

At night, and until the early morning, tawny owls call in Fairyland, and sometimes on the Granny Downs.

Most trees are bare, although some small beeches retain their dead leaves and these rattle in the wind.

Silver birches reach their golden finest days before gales steal the leaves: now, new catkins on the bare twigs clutch the air like grappling hooks. Fresh growth on the limes gives them a warm, red outline, and the bobbled fruits of the plane trees hang like Christmas decorations.

Berries are welcome points of colour: this old hawthorn has dark red berries on its twigs like details on fine oriental china. Further down the branch, thick bunches of lichen look like pale green seaweed.

Fungi surprise. Perfectly disguised amidst the fallen leaves of a sessile oak on the Zoo Banks, I find a colony of lilac fungi: these are called *charcoal burner*. Fungi have a wealth of graphic names.

In the middle of the month, the Geminid meteor shower bursts into the night sky and the Downs is a sufficiently dark and wide arena in which to see the silent fireworks. A meteor is a flash of light produced when a particle of space dust enters our atmosphere: Geminid meteors are produced by debris from the asteroid Phaethon. The shooting stars peak during the nights of the 13th and 14th December and we can see them if the sky is clear.

Geminid meteors are slow and graceful and we have time to relish them. On the Downs, the silver light disturbs the birds and some twitter briefly after each shooting star.

I first saw the Geminids on a frosty morning before dawn as I waited near the Seven Sisters, and I felt alone on a planet in infinity. But I wished I had taken an overcoat and flask of tea.

Sweet violets begin to bud, near Ladies Mile: there is usually a show of them in flower on Christmas Day.

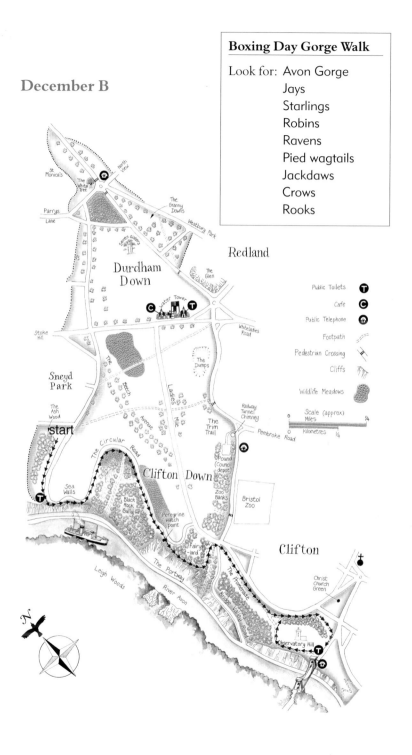

Boxing Day Gorge Walk

Look for: Avon Gorge
Jays
Starlings
Robins
Ravens
Pied wagtails
Jackdaws
Crows
Rooks

December B

St Monica's

North View

The White Tree

Parrys Lane

The Granny Downs

Westbury Park

Seven Sisters

Redland

Durdham Down

The Glen

Water Tower

Whiteladies Road

Stoke Hill

The Beech

The Dumps

Sneyd Park

Ladies Mile

The Ash Wood

Avenue

Railway Tunnel Chimney

Pembroke Road

The Trim Trail

start

The Circular Road

Pound (Council depot)

Sea Walls

Clifton Down

Black Rock Gully

Zoo Banks

Bristol Zoo

Peregrine watch point

Fairy-land

Clifton

Leigh Woods

The Portway

River Avon

Christ Church Green

Clifton Suspension Bridge

Bridge Valley Road

The Promenade

Observatory Hill

Public Toilets T
Cafe C
Public Telephone

Footpath

Pedestrian Crossing

Cliffs

Wildlife Meadows

Scale (approx)
Miles   1/4
0
Kilometres   1/4
0

N

Index

Bold numbers refer to the write ups for individual species.